Collected Poems

MERVYN PEAKE was one of the best-loved illustrators of the twentieth century, and author of the celebrated Titus books: *Titus Groan* (1946), *Gormenghast* (1950) and *Titus Alone* (1959). Born in China in 1911, he was educated at Tientsin Grammar School, Eltham College in Kent and the Royal Academy Schools. From 1935 he taught life drawing at the Westminster School of Art. After being called up in 1940 he underwent military training, but was invalided out of the army following a breakdown in 1942. He worked for a while as an official War Artist, then in 1945 travelled through Germany recording the after-effects of the war, making drawings of Nazi war criminals, POWs and the concentration camp at Bergen-Belsen. In 1946 he went with his family to live on the remote island of Sark, returning in 1949 to teach life drawing again, this time at the Central School of Art. He was awarded the Heinemann Prize by the Royal Society of Literature in 1951 for his novel *Gormenghast* and poetry collection *The Glassblowers*. His play *The Wit to Woo* was performed at the Arts Theatre in 1957 but did not prove a critical success, and he suffered a second breakdown after its failure. He was diagnosed with Parkinson's disease in 1958, and died ten years later.

R.W. MASLEN is Senior Lecturer at the University of Glasgow. His publications include *Elizabethan Fictions* (1997), *Shakespeare and Comedy* (2005) and an edition of Philip Sidney's *Apology for Poetry* (2002). He has also written a number of essays on Elizabethan literature and twentieth-century fantasy.

Fyfield*Books* aim to make available some of the great classics of British and European literature in clear, affordable formats, and to restore often neglected writers to their place in literary tradition.

Fyfield*Books* take their name from the Fyfield elm in Matthew Arnold's 'Scholar Gypsy' and 'Thyrsis'. The tree stood not far from the village where the series was originally devised in 1971.

> *Roam on! The light we sought is shining still.*
> *Dost thou ask proof? Our tree yet crowns the hill,*
> *Our Scholar travels yet the loved hill-side*

from 'Thyrsis'

MERVYN PEAKE

Collected Poems

Edited with an introduction by
R.W. MASLEN

Fyfield*Books*

CARCANET

First published in Great Britain in 2008 by
Carcanet Press Limited
Alliance House
Cross Street
Manchester M2 7AQ

A CIP catalogue record for this book is available from the British Library
ISBN 978 1 85754 971 3

The publisher acknowledges financial assistance from Arts Council England

Typeset by XL Publishing Services, Tiverton
Printed and bound in England by SRP Ltd, Exeter

Contents

Illustrations

Dates indicate when a drawing was executed, unless preceded by the word 'published'.

Acknowledgements

This edition has been made possible by the extraordinary generosity of four people. First, Michael Schmidt, whose enthusiasm for the project got it off the ground and carried it through to completion. Next, Sebastian Peake of the Mervyn Peake Estate, whose excitement at the prospect of seeing his father's poetry in print has been more than matched by his kindness in sending me huge numbers of photocopies; welcoming me into his flat to read his father's manuscripts; and responding with unfailing courtesy to my endless queries as work progressed. Thirdly, the world's foremost Peake scholar, G. Peter Winnington, has given liberally of his time and expertise, as well as inviting me to his house in Switzerland for a weekend's intensive deciphering of manuscripts, punctuated by walks in the fabulous Jura. His e-mails were packed with valuable information and advice, including manuscripts, typescripts and crucial suggestions as to the dating of Peake's verse. Without his on-line resource 'A Title and First-Line Index to Peake's Poems' the project would have taken years rather than months to complete. Fourthly, Alison Eldred has spent hours seeking out and making copies of Peake's illustrations for me, as well as photocopying his verse. Her cheerful professionalism in scanning and safely mailing CDs full of pictures has cut further years from the process of putting all these items together. There's no way of thanking these four adequately, except by assuring them that this edition is more theirs than mine.

Thanks to Pete Bellotte, who found the poem 'Birth of Day' in the correspondence of Gordon Smith; and to the Department of English Literature at the University of Glasgow, which funded my trip to Switzerland to consult Peter Winnington and paid for a subscription to his essential journal *Peake Studies*.

Warm thanks to Judith Willson at Carcanet for her hard work at every stage of the project. Thanks too to Mr Colin Harris and Dr Judith Priestman at the Bodleian Library, Oxford, and the staff at the library of University College, London. Brook and Zhenya

Horowitz, Michael Piret, and my brother and sister-in-law, Tom and Sam Maslen, put me up while I was working in the Peake archives at UCL and Oxford; affectionate thanks to all of them, and to Brandon and Gabriel for their stimulating company in High Wycombe.

Julie Martis set me off on the trail that led to this edition in October 2006, when she asked where she could get hold of Peake's poems after seeing a picture of Steerpike on my wall. Thanks to her for the inquiry; I hope she approves of the book that came out of it.

Finally, thank you to Kirsty, Bethany and Grace for being with me – though not always physically – while I worked. Every bit of this that's mine is dedicated to them.

R.W. Maslen
2008

Introduction

This book will come as something of a revelation. Even those readers who are most familiar with Peake's work can have had little idea he wrote so much poetry. They will be surprised all over again that so much of his unpublished verse should turn out to be so good. And they will be surprised for a third time that so many poems they thought they knew should look so different in the versions given here. 'Heaven lures me', for instance, has become 'Heaven hires me' (p. 30), transforming what was once a tale of celestial seduction into a meditation on unearthly employment. 'Sneers the cock eagle' has become 'Sheers the cock eagle' (p. 59), so that the formerly earthbound raptor has taken flight; and 'The Time Has Come for More than Small Decisions' is now 'Before Man's Bravery I Bow My Head' (p. 90), the consequence of a rearrangement of the poem's structure. The long poem 'A Reverie of Bone' has acquired seven new stanzas (pp. 106–15). Each of these compositions has been given an approximate date. And each now stands surrounded by unfamiliar verse, some of which may change the way we think of Peake for ever.

Many of these innovations were made possible by an event of the kind every editor dreams of: the discovery of two previously unknown notebooks, into which Peake transcribed or pasted drafts and fair copies of his verses over several years. The first notebook has no cover, and he probably stopped using it in 1939. It includes drawings of Peake's mother on her deathbed in October of that year, a number of poems about the imminent outbreak of war, and no drawings at all of Peake's son Sebastian, who was born in January 1940 and images of whose face immediately began to fill every bit of scrap paper his father could lay hands on. The second notebook has a red cover and is more difficult to date. The last few pages contain sketches for the dust jacket of Peake's novel *Titus Groan*, which was published in 1946, and a few notes on the writing of the book which look as if they were made for publicity purposes. There is also a note listing what seems to be work needing completion or just completed: this includes the dust jacket of his children's book *Letters from a Lost Uncle*, published in 1948 but possibly written as early as 1945, and a set of five nonsense poems and pictures written and drawn for a new periodical in 1946. The indications are, then, that the notebook dates from no later than 1946, and this is supported by the apparent age of Peake's sons in the many sketches of them it contains.

Thanks to these notebooks and other findings, there are over 230 poems in this edition: so many, in fact, that I have been forced to leave out one long poem from his adolescence ('The Touch o' the Ash', which you can read in *Peake's Progress*, pp. 45–61) and all his nonsense verse (some of which can be read in *A Book of Nonsense*). More than eighty of these poems have never before appeared in print. The rest were scattered across a wide range of publications, from the four poetry collections printed in his lifetime – only two of which he was able to see through the press – to the pages of journals, the four posthumous collections, and the miscellany *Peake's Progress*. Putting all these poems together gives us a book of real substance. It's as if we had found a new Gormenghast manuscript tucked away behind one of Peake's canvases: a manuscript filled with clues to the many points of contact between his private imaginative world and the world of bloodshed and enraptured creativity, propaganda and modernist experiment, military discipline and bohemianism, conservatism and technological innovation, together with the traumas induced by the shocking collisions between all these things, which Peake and his contemporaries were condemned to inhabit.

In fact, this book marks the emergence of a significant new poet of the mid-twentieth century. Peake's stature as a writer of verse first won recognition in 1951, when he received the Heinemann Prize jointly for his novel *Gormenghast* and his second collection of poetry, *The Glassblowers*. By that time his poems had appeared in some of the most prestigious magazines of the day, such as *The Listener*, *The Spectator* and *New English Weekly* – the magazine that published much of the early verse of his friend Dylan Thomas. Between 1972 and 1981 Peake's *Selected Poems* was printed three times by Faber and Faber, and John Batchelor wrote a glowing appreciation of his poetry in his book *Mervyn Peake: A Biographical and Critical Exploration* (1974). But since the early 1980s his achievements in verse have been eclipsed by the rapid rise of his reputation as a novelist and illustrator. The growing international market for his drawings and paintings, the BBC adaptation of *Gormenghast* for television in 2000 which alerted readers outside Britain to the existence of the Titus books, the eloquent enthusiasm expressed for those books by writers of fantastic fiction whose own stature has grown incrementally since the 70s – Michael Moorcock, Angela Carter, M. John Harrison, Neil Gaiman, not to mention Anthony Burgess and Robertson Davies – these things have paradoxically overwhelmed the claim of Peake's poetry to serious attention. Besides, nobody until now has had any idea of the sheer *scale* of his poetic output: its ambitiousness, its imaginative coherence, its linguistic and rhythmic inventiveness. With this edition, his achievement as a poet can at last be fairly assessed. And as the Heinemann judges recognised, that achievement is considerable.

Peake wrote verse compulsively from his teenage years (an example from 1929 is given here) to the publication of *The Glassblowers* in 1950; and although his output diminished in the 50s, he continued to write plays in verse throughout that decade. The manuscripts of the Titus books – especially the first – are peppered with verse, scribbled at the back of the exercise books in which he was drafting and redrafting his prose narratives. And Gormenghast itself resounds with poetry: from the mournful rhymes declaimed by the castle poet when he pokes his head out of a window during Steerpike's giddy scramble over the rooftops of the building, to the interminable verses recited by another poet at a party in *Titus Alone* (1959). The Titus books are often described as 'poetic' by their admirers: a recognition of the rhythmic, metaphorical and syntactical inventiveness of their prose, which sometimes settles into regular metre, as in the ravings of the mad Lord Sepulchrave in *Titus Groan*, whose iambic cadences resemble fragments of the Jacobean tragedies he may once have kept in his burnt-out library. When in 1957 Peake succumbed to the illness that killed him eleven years later – an illness that meant he could no longer write prose or drama – he continued to generate verse of remarkable power. He was a poet to his backbone, and it was as a visionary painter-poet that he first cherished ambitions to be remembered. 'I am almost drunken with an arrogant / Madness of desire to follow in the line / Of England's poets', he wrote at the age of twenty-eight (p. 65), and his passion for 'mysterious words / Of deep and coloured music' never left him.

His verse charts the relationship between his astonishing imaginative life and the turbulent times he lived in more intimately than any biography (and we are lucky enough to have had no less than seven biographies and book-length memoirs of Peake since his death). By presenting its contents in roughly chronological order, this edition enables us to trace the development of his poetic talent through his lifetime, and to see how he worked to nurture that talent. We can see, too, how he kept returning to certain burning questions: by what means a verbal or visual craftsman achieves the 'miracle' of creation; the nature of the visceral response he had to beauty, which mingled terror and torment with delight; the problem of reconciling his wish to be a responsible artist with the fundamentally amoral process of generating a work of art, especially at a time of global warfare. Much of his poetry concerns itself with the impulse to 'fashion bright and timeless things / In the chilly shadow of war's wings' (as he puts it in 'The Sullen Accents Told of Doom', p. 89). The sense that creativity and destructiveness, love and aggression painfully co-exist in human beings is one of the perceptions he repeatedly recast in new poetic terms, before and after the war as well as during it.

What this edition cannot show us, however, is how thoroughly Peake revised his verse. His manuscripts are seamed with scorings-out, and criss-crossed with alternative lines or words – many of them not cancelled, so that in the case of unpublished poems it is often hard to tell which version of a given line, which word, Peake might finally have preferred among the several alternatives he scribbled side by side. Even after printing Peake revised his poems, altering them – in some cases radically – in the journey from magazine to book. He was a meticulous worker, which is no doubt what drew him so often to the subject of work: Welsh miners in 'Rhondda Valley' (p. 27), digging soldiers in 'The Spadesmen' (p. 90), skilled craftsmen in 'The Glassblowers' (p. 125). 'We do not see with our eyes but with our trades,' he said in a radio talk of 1947. As a result, every trade fascinated him, from the sailor's to those of the minister, the doctor or the scrubber of a kitchen floor. He loved to imagine his way into new trades so as to obtain new angles for the 'tiny lens' (his term for the organ of vision in 'Where Got I These Two Eyes that Plunder Storm', p. 56). One such trade was that of the poet, and he laboured long and hard to fashion himself into a fine one.

It is important, though, to point out that many of the poems in this edition never went through the lengthy process of redrafting from which his finished work benefited. Some read, in fact, like verbal counterparts to the thousands of sketches an artist must produce if he is to keep his hand in – like the drawings Peake made while wandering the streets of London in the 1930s and 40s on his 'headhunting' expeditions, ceaselessly recording the faces he saw in cafés, bars, dancehalls and buses. His verse can have the same unfinished quality as these drawings, the same concern with returning to some question of form or substance obsessively until he has articulated it to his satisfaction. Examples might be the two poems about a fearsome visionary moment, 'I Found Myself Walking' (p. 73) and 'Suddenly, Walking along the Open Road' (p. 116), which describe two similar incidents in different words and were never printed in his lifetime; or 'Sensitive Head' (p. 53), which tells of an encounter with a stranger, perhaps while 'head-hunting'. As with visual sketches, these verbal ones may be found to have an energy that's lost to the polished final version; and some try out new techniques he never made part of his 'stock and store' (a phrase from the verse sketch 'To a Scarecrow Gunner', p. 85). For this reason I've included several fragmentary pieces in this book, some of which are as evocative as anything he wrote.

In his trade as a visual artist, Peake worked successfully in a wide range of media, paying close attention to the peculiar qualities of the materials he used. His oils exploit the plasticity of paint; his Chinese brush drawings sensuously respond to the thickening and thinning of the brush as it sweeps across the paper; his cross-hatched pen-and-ink illustrations delight in the different textures imparted to a picture's surface by a change in the direction or pressure of the many small strokes of the pen's sharp nib; his pencil sketches indulge the interplay of softness and sharpness made available by the altering shape of the lead. One can see the same intense delight in the resources of language in his poetry. He exulted in the music of words, in their shapes on the page as well as their sounds in the ear, and was always in quest of new adjectives and nouns to add to his verbal palette. According to his friend Gordon Smith, he quarried *Roget's Thesaurus* for unfamiliar terms with which to 'Enrich' the 'Wild heritage' of the English tongue (a practice Peake seems to invoke in the poem 'Into the Dusky Well', p. 158). When writing about drawing – as he did with unrivalled lyricism – he expressed his creative process as a visual artist in poetic terms, speaking passionately about the need for 'rhythm' in a pencil sketch, about how a line can be seen as an utterance, about how the artist's quest for a style is a lifelong journey 'to discover his language'. For him, the creative processes of generating verse sprang from the same internal sources that produce a picture, and nobody has sought with more commitment to find a vocabulary for those creative processes than Peake.

Thinking about Peake's poetry in terms of his visual art, then, can be helpful. Although he is famous for writing and drawing fantastic things – the Titus books are about life in a gargantuan, self-sufficient castle, his illustrations are of fairy tales, ancient mariners and Snarks – he was throughout his life a master of life drawing, teaching it in a succession of art schools, obsessively sketching the bodies, clothed and unclothed, of his wife Maeve and their three children. His fantasies, in other words, are anchored to the solid framework of the bone – something he dazzlingly demonstrated in his long verse meditation on the human skeleton, 'A Reverie of Bone' (pp. 106–15). The reverie of the poem's title is a trance state induced by prolonged staring at femurs, ribs and vertebrae; in his essay *The Craft of the Lead Pencil* (1946) Peake writes at length on the importance of the *stare* in drawing from life. For him, proper staring produces an effect somewhat akin to being possessed; an absorption of your subject, so that in a sense you *become* that subject, feeling and thinking like him or her (or it, in the case of a bone) irrespective of social or ethical considerations. Staring can lead to a spontaneous outbreak of affection, as in the poem 'Sensitive Head', where the steady contemplation of an unknown man in a café is said to have 'Stopped my heart / With love' (p. 53). But there can also be something frightening about its effect on the starer. The will to possess and be possessed by an object just because it excites you aesthetically presents a challenge to easy systems of morality. One of Peake's wartime poems speaks of the 'Beauty' prized by artist and writer as 'Dead to our values', being born even at a time when 'The murderous army… Is dark on the skyline' (p. 72). The hammering dactyls drive home the urgent eroticism of the 'need' the poet feels for this 'Terrible, sheer, / Omnipresent, unfailing / God', despite its unsettling resistance to the recognised methods of evaluation.

In 1940 Peake drew a series of pictures purporting to derive from the portfolio of 'Adolf Hitler, Artist' (two of them are reproduced in this book, pp. 83 and 88). Each picture carries a conventional title ('Study of a Young Girl', 'Still Life', 'Landscape with Figures', 'Mother and Child'); but each records an atrocity. The young girl has been shot in the breast, the landscape shows refugees dragging themselves wearily through a bombed-out city, the agonised mother holds a baby whose head has been smashed by shrapnel. The self-portrait of Hitler that fronts the series shows him staring out of the page with huge, horrified eyes and sweat-covered face, appalled at the task he has set himself of exhibiting his own face alongside those of his victims. Peake's poems suggest that he shared with this imaginary Hitler a profound horror at the concept of making art from the devastation of the Second World War – even though Peake could not be held personally accountable for that devastation. Twice at least he wrote poems whose lines come into existence at the precise moment when human existences elsewhere are being snuffed out. 'Is There No Love Can Link Us?' (p. 103) seeks to find something more than mere simultaneity to connect the writer with the men, women and children who are 'dying now, this moment as I write / And may be cold before this line's complete'. And the fragment 'If I Would Stay What Men Call Sane' (p. 123) – written after his breakdown in 1942 – expresses both his need to turn away from the war's obscenities ('Lord / Save me from my Imagination's Truth') and his distaste for the 'slurring brain'

> That cannot dare to realize, that now
> Now, now, the bomb strikes, and flung limbs are strewn
> Severed and fresh since this short poem started.

In each case, the artist's uncompromising 'stare' makes his verse absorb and thus in a sense become complicit with the monstrous moments it registers. In 'Had Each a Voice What Would His Fingers Cry' (p. 95), an artist who has been drafted into the army, like Peake himself, finds his own digits rebelling against their new occupation, and accusing his brain of 'treachery' for consenting to participate in the grim artistry of rifle practice. Savage self-criticism, an internal civil war, dominate Peake's wartime verses, in a dreadful pastiche of the productive self-criticism all creative minds must cultivate.

Peake's uncanny ability to make rich verse out of war-damage continued to haunt him after the war, and only got purged from his system when he composed, in about 1947, his visionary ballad 'The Rhyme of the Flying Bomb' (pp. 178–201). Unpublished at the time – as if writing it was enough – the ballad is filled with a ghastly exultation at the sublime beauty of the Blitz, as well as with protests at the necessity of living through this dire moment in history. Above all, the poem insists on the *innocence* of the two figures it follows through the blazing London streets. One is a newborn baby, which can speak and has inhabited this world in some previous existence, yet remains untraumatised by the terrors visited on it in its successive lives. The other is a sailor, who seems to have been lifted wholesale from the sea-stories Peake loved as a boy. His mode of speech and the diction used to describe him recall a book Peake knew by heart, Stevenson's *Treasure Island*, so that the sailor's very fictionality absolves him of guilt for the bombardment of London. His boyish amazement at the fire-ravaged cityscape underscores his guiltlessness, as does the fact that he is associated with water, not fire, and therefore utterly divorced from the element in which he finds himself (like the baby, which he addresses as 'little fish'). In this way Peake liberated himself from the demons of self-accusation that had possessed his imagination for so long.

But *failing* to connect with war and its victims was as horrifying a prospect for Peake as being possessed by them. His famous poem 'The Consumptive. Belsen 1945' (p. 133) expresses shock at his own callous reaction to a dying girl he saw in the hospital for concentration camp inmates at Bergen-Belsen. In her face he notes the seeds of a 'great painting', and as he mentally nurtures these seeds he finds himself unable to respond as he should to the girl's suffering. Filled with remorse, he promises in the penultimate line that her dying 'shall not be betrayed', presumably by being trans-formed into a work of art. Yet by then the work of art has already come into being: it is the poem we have just read. A similar absence of sympathy is confessed in the 1941 poem 'What Is It Muffles the Ascending Moment?' (p. 95), where the poet watches the Blitz as if 'Through darkened glass', unable to internalise the torment of its victims. And in 'Is There No Love Can Link Us?' (p. 103), the only link the poet can find between himself and the dying citizens of London is 'this sliding / Second we share: this desperate edge of now'. The desperate days of war are also (as he writes in 'Yet Who to Love Returning', p. 136) the 'disparate days', when emotions are dulled and the one sure bond we share is not with the living but the 'horizontal dead' ('The Two Fraternities', p. 86), who have lost all feeling.

The failure to connect – to be really present at a significant point in time – was something Peake wrote about occasionally before the war, as in 'Poem: Body and head and arms and throat and hands' (p. 39), where a pair of lovers find themselves unexpectedly detached from one another at the moment of meeting: 'But where are you? And I? Am I with me?' At the height of war, though, Peake's guilty sense of detachment from other people's pain seems to have affected his relationship with his wife Maeve for a prolonged period. Just before his nervous breakdown in 1942 he wrote: 'Your face, made in your likeness, / Floats like a ghost through its own clay from me, / Even from you – O it has left us, we / Are parted by a tract of thorn and water' (p. 118). Here Maeve's face resembles a sculpture that somehow disconnects its viewers from the woman in whose likeness it was made. The same notion of the work of art as both a representation of alienation and a cause of estrangement is developed in the poem 'Half-Light' (p. 166), where Maeve briefly becomes a 'carving' whose 'strange beauty' cuts Peake off from her, until her smile calls him back from 'a region that was fierce and lonely'. Art, then, can either forge bonds between artist/viewer and subject or else divorce them from one another. This is in part because the writer-artist has at once a desperate need to communicate and a need for detachment, for solitude in which to observe, imagine and create. In 'Half-Light', Peake's return from his temporary alienation from Maeve involves her 'Tearing tremendous wings from off my back' – violently plucking him from the state of imaginative rapture that enabled him to see her in statuesque 'glory'. His restoration to her necessitates, it seems, a loss of inspiration, an arrest of the Pegasus-like flight that took him beyond any love for or even engagement with her. Peake's creative energy springs from an interior space which finally nobody – not even he himself – can fully penetrate; and this is one reason why his poetry as well as his prose so freely mixes the fantastic things of the private imagination with material things and people: centaurs, satyrs and angels with glassblowers, trees and aeroplanes. It is also why so much of his work is preoc-cupied with loneliness, even when its ostensible subject is love.

Peake emerges from this edition, then, as a pre-eminent war poet; but there is much more here than the poetry of violence. John Batchelor indicated the range of Peake's preoccupations when he discussed his verse under several headings: 'head-hunting' poems, 'inward' poems, love poems, mystical poems and romantic poems, as well as poems of war. Peake himself in his 1946 note-book made lists of headings under which his verse might be assembled: love poems and poems of wartime, poems of dejection and of ego, objective poems, nature poems, abstract poems. He wrote, too, a series of responses to the artists he admired: the Parisian artist Mané Katz (p. 34), El Greco (p. 41), Van Gogh (p. 44), Jacob Epstein, whose statue of Adam he defended in 1939 (p. 45), William Blake (p. 63), and the poet Robert Frost (p. 169). And he penned many pieces about his own artistic aspirations, such as the early 'Coloured Money' (p. 22) and 'Heaven Hires Me' (p. 30), which are filled with economic metaphors that foreshadow his lifelong struggle to make ends meet as an artist, and the antagonism this instilled in him towards the values of a capitalist society; an antagonism most fully expressed in the unpolished poem 'I Sing a Hatred of the Black Machine' (c. 1939) (pp. 67–8), where capitalism and the rise of jack-booted Nazism become one in the wilful damage they do to art. The sentiment found more succinct expression in one of Peake's best pieces, 'To Live at All Is Miracle Enough' (c. 1949; p. 207), which exudes a Blake-like conviction that painters and poets can triumphantly assert their independence in the face of the industrial, financial and military pressure-groups that seek to commandeer their services. Both 'I Sing a Hatred' and 'To Live at All' identify armed conflict as merely the most appalling manifestation of an ongoing struggle between the artist who 'labours at a work he loves' and the 'clanky fortresses of greed' sustained by alienated labour. His third Titus book, *Titus Alone* (1959), translates this notion into the medium of prose satire – though its prose is always on the verge of mutating into the metre of his earlier assaults on capitalism.

For all its diversity, Peake's verse – and indeed his prose – has as its default setting the commonest metre in English poetry, the iambic pentameter: the ten-syllable, five-stress line of the Renaissance playwrights he so admired. His biographer John Watney tells us that he used to stride around his house reciting great swathes of Marlowe's *Tamburlaine*; and one of Peake's earliest and most murderous creations, Mr Slaughterboard, has a complete set of the Elizabethan dramatists, bound in vellum, on board his ship. Sometimes Peake falls into the ballad rhythms cultivated by Keats and Coleridge, and his early poetry is affected by the sprung rhythm of Hopkins and Dylan Thomas; but one can hear an iambic music struggling to assert itself behind even the freest of his verses. Partly as a result of this, his poems are filled with strong echoes of the great poems he knew so well. Milton's sonnet on his blindness is transformed into a poem on another visionary, Blake: 'When I remember how his spirit throve / Amid dark city streets he did not see' (p. 63). Donne resonates through the unfinished poem 'For God's Sake Draw the Blind' (p. 227); Shakespeare's Henry V is there in the line 'And at his heels are hunger's restless hounds' (p. 203); and Hopkins's sonnets feed into the sonnet on an aeroplane, 'Where Skidded Only in the Upper Air' (p. 50). Coleridge's *Ancient Mariner* is everywhere in 'The Rhyme of the Flying Bomb'. But Peake's contemporaries, too, find their work embedded in his. Eliot's 'The Hollow Men' becomes a meditation on the poet's helplessness in the approach to war in 'We Are the Haunted People' (p. 48), while Dylan Thomas's most political poem, 'The hand that signed the paper', is rendered Gothic in 'Crumbles the Crested Scroll' (p. 147). Yeats's 'Sailing to Byzantium' inhabits 'Swans Die and a Tower Falls' (p. 176). Peake knew and admired the work of Auden, Frost, MacNeice, Spender, James Stephens and Vernon Watkins, among many others, as well as the poetic prose of Joyce and Woolf; and he enjoyed a lasting friendship with Walter de la Mare. He was, then, as aware of the traditions he wrote in as of the way the modernists sought to disrupt and renew them; hence the archaisms that lend an air of weird antiquity to his verse, even as it encounters the most urgently current issues. Like other modernist works, his poetic representations of twentieth-century life throw up shattered fragments of earlier centuries in new shapes, mimicking the bombed-out buildings he wrote about with such tenderness.

In the introduction to his book of drawings (1947), Peake speaks of the 'authority' of a drawing, which it derives from 'its overtones and echoes which show it to be borne rapidly or languorously along one of the deep streams that wind back through time to a cave in Spain'. 'The repercussions of the dead', he goes on, 'disturb the page; an aeon of ghosts float by with charcoal in their hands.' This is certainly true of Peake's illustrations, which summon up the ghosts both of the text they embellish and of earlier illustrators: Gustave Doré stands behind Peake's version of the *Ancient Mariner*, John Tenniel and Henry Holiday behind his illustrations to the works of Carroll. And his poems, too, rewrite the canon in terms of searing immediacy. Their confrontation of the atrocities of their day with the archaic 'deep streams that wind back through time' is what gives them their strangeness and their power. They are the verbal equivalent of illustrations, answering back to other people's words as dynamically as his drawings did.

But there is more to his poems than the clash of ancient and modern, or stirring echoes of well-known poetic voices. Writing to Gordon Smith – who did more than anyone else to encourage his versifying – Peake described an effect he wanted to achieve in the first of his Titus novels. 'I mean', he wrote, 'that the mood should be always, although I hope varied from chapter to chapter – yet consistently, say, Gryphon, and not Bulldog, Gazelle or even Gargoyle. Always Gryphon (par exemple) – a gryphon that may have a complex temperament and show different coloured scales under different lights – but whose smell must pervade every page – sometimes like Gryphonodour, sometimes Gryphonstench – sometimes Gryphon-of-roses.' Peake's poetry, even from the first, has an atmosphere, a music, a smell even, all of its own. It is easy to believe that one would recognise a poem of his at once, even if it were published anonymously. Varied though they are, and self-evidently products of a 'complex temperament', his verses cohere as a body into a being that seems larger than the sum of its parts – very much like Gormenghast castle. I hope the present volume will ensure that this being shuffles into place at last among the other vexed, idiosyncratic art-works of the cataclysmic time in which he lived.

A Note on the Text

Mervyn Peake revised his work extensively, so that several versions exist of many of his poems. Where possible, I have reproduced the latest version he is known to have overseen himself. Where it is not known which is the latest version, I have chosen the one that seems most coherent.

Peake only saw two volumes of poetry through the press: *Shapes and Sounds* (1941) and *The Glassblowers* (1950). I have reproduced the contents of these volumes as accurately as I could. Where verses he sent to a magazine represent the latest version of a given poem, I have reproduced these faithfully, too.

Poems that appear in the two notebooks mentioned in the introduction are also reproduced accurately, but with occasional slight adjustments to spelling and punctuation. Peake had a relaxed attitude to both these matters, which he tended to correct in the final revision. Where possible, I have modified punctuation with reference to other extant drafts or typescripts of the poem; but here or there I have introduced punctuation of my own where I feel it is necessary to make a text readable. All such additions are indicated in the notes. In many cases I have left poems as lightly punctuated as they are in the sources, either because they seem to me more effective like this or because they are clearly less 'finished' drafts than the more carefully transcribed MS poems. I hope my decision not to add punctuation will be considered no more presumptuous than my decision to put it in.

The Peake Estate has also made available to me a number of loose-leaf manuscripts and typescripts. I have treated the manuscripts as I treated the notebooks – though it should be said that Peake's minuscule handwriting isn't always easy to decipher. The typescripts are trickier to deal with. Peake could type, but he also made use of professional typists. So too did his wife Maeve when editing his work after the onset of his last illness. Some typescripts have been carefully amended in Peake's hand; these I take to be authoritative. Others are full of gobbledygook, evidently the result of misreading manuscripts. Misreading is especially easy where Peake has jotted down several alternatives for a word, phrase or line without indicating which he prefers. As a result, some poems were originally published with one or more extra lines, or with extra words in a line – the consequence of choosing more than one alternative. In most cases I have been able to correct such misreadings by reference to a manuscript or to a typescript corrected by Peake; but very occasionally I have had to make an educated guess at a misreading that has taken place. The most extreme example of this is 'Staring in Madness' (p. 227). The notes indicate where such guesswork has been necessary.

Where manuscripts give two or more alternatives without indicating a preference, I have felt justified in choosing the alternative I prefer. In most cases this seems to be the latest thought Peake had on a subject. He was an astute reviser of his verse.

'The Rhyme of the Flying Bomb' is reproduced from the first edition, with some punctuation added from the version in the 1981 corrected edition of *Peake's Progress*. It should be noted that Peake did not see this poem through the press himself, and that no manuscript is known to exist apart from some early drafts in the Bodleian Library.

Most of the dates given in this edition are approximate; I have indicated in the notes how they were arrived at. In each case they represent the earliest date by which we can be reasonably sure a poem was written. It should be stressed that the dates given for previously unpublished verse in the two notebooks are for the most part no more than the probable date when Peake finished compiling the relevant notebook; some of these poems were obviously composed some time beforehand.

Further Reading

This is a partial list; a full bibliography, which includes details of all works cited in this *Collected Poems,* can be found at the website of the journal *Peake Studies* under the heading 'Peake in Print' (peakestudies.com/contents.htm). This includes an authoritative 'Title and First-Line Index to Peake's Poems'.

Editions

Shapes and Sounds (London: Chatto and Windus, 1941)
Rhymes Without Reason (London: Eyre and Spottiswoode, 1944)
Titus Groan (London: Eyre and Spottiswoode, 1946)
Letters from a Lost Uncle (from Polar Regions) (London: Eyre and Spottiswoode, 1948)
Drawings by Mervyn Peake (London: Grey Walls Press, 1949)
The Glassblowers (London: Eyre and Spottiswoode, 1950)
Gormenghast (London: Eyre and Spottiswoode, 1950)
Titus Alone (London: Eyre and Spottiswoode, 1959)
The Rhyme of the Flying Bomb (London: Dent, 1962)
Poems and Drawings (Richmond, Surrey: Keepsake Press, 1965)
A Reverie of Bone (London: Bertram Rota, 1967)
Selected Poems (London: Faber and Faber, 1972)
A Book of Nonsense (London: Peter Owen, 1972)
Writings and Drawings, ed. Maeve Gilmore and Shelagh Johnson (London and New York: Academy Editions/St Martin's Press, 1974)
Twelve Poems (London: Mervyn Peake Society, 1975)
Peake's Progress, ed. Maeve Gilmore (London: Allen Lane, 1978; second edition with corrections by G. Peter Winnington, Harmondsworth: Penguin, 1981)
Ten Poems (London: Mervyn Peake Society, 1993)
Eleven Poems (London: Mervyn Peake Society, 1995)

Biographies and Memoirs

Batchelor, John, *Mervyn Peake: A Biographical and Critical Exploration* (London: Duckworth, 1974)

Gilmore, Maeve, *A World Away: A Memoir of Mervyn Peake* (London: Victor Gollancz, 1970)

Peake, Sebastian, *A Child of Bliss: Growing Up with Mervyn Peake* (Oxford: Lennard, 1989)

Smith, Gordon, *Mervyn Peake: A Personal Memoir* (London: Victor Gollancz, 1984)

Watney, John, *Mervyn Peake* (London: Michael Joseph, 1976)

Winnington, G. Peter, *Vast Alchemies: The Life and Work of Mervyn Peake* (London and Chester Springs: Peter Owen, 2000)

Yorke, Malcolm, *Mervyn Peake: My Eyes Mint Gold: A Life* (London: John Murray, 2000)

Criticism

Batchelor, John, *Mervyn Peake: A Biographical and Critical Exploration*. Chapter 10, 'The Poems', gives one of the few detailed appraisals of Peake's verse, describing Peake as 'a good… neo-romantic poet' and identifying 'The Glassblowers' as the finest of his poems.

—— 'Mervyn Peake, Poet', in *Peake Papers*, ed. by various hands (London: Mervyn Peake Society, 1994), pp. 5–16.

Le Guin, Ursula K., *'Peake's Progress*, by Mervyn Peake', *Dancing at the Edge of the World: Thoughts on Words, Women, Places* (New York etc.: Harper and Row, 1989), pp. 273–5. This short review by one of the other great writers of twentieth-century fantasy celebrates his poetry as of 'extraordinary power and brilliance', singling out 'The Rhyme of the Flying Bomb' and 'London, 1941' for special praise.

Piette, Adam, *The Imagination at War: British Fiction and Poetry, 1939–1945* (London and Basingstoke: Macmillan, 1995), pp. 49–54. Piette does not discuss Peake's poetry, but he recognises Peake's articulation in *Titus Groan* of 'the dark nature of the Blitz for many Londoners: as revelatory of their own self-destructive desires and death-wishes – a kind of psychic civil war'. His perceptions are directly relevant to Peake's verse.

Smith, Gordon, *Mervyn Peake: A Personal Memoir*. The section headed 'Achievements' identifies 'The Rhyme of the Flying Bomb' as 'one of the great war-poems'.

Spender, Stephen, 'Poetry in 1941', *Horizon*, vol. 5, no. 26 (February 1942), pp. 96–111. Describes Peake's poetry as 'technically weak' but the work of 'a remarkably sincere and intelligent person'.

Winnington, G. Peter, *The Voice of the Heart: The Working of Mervyn Peake's Imagination* (Liverpool: Liverpool University Press, 2006). This is the most important critical work on Peake. Every chapter contains brilliant insights directly relevant to his poetry.

The Poems

Birth of Day

Th'invisible scimitar of Morn,
Again had passionately torn
And slashed the Sky's pale neck;
Way down aye far within that East
Where paleness reigns, and pale stars cease
The Sky's wide bowl to deck.

There where the long and cruel blade
Within those livid heavens had made
Its deep sweeps, in the Sky –
Blood in the gashes, welled; and grew;
Intensified; diffused; and blue
Slate coloured clouds stole by.

Above those dark and sepia hills –
Intensely deep, the Great Sky thrills
In a welter of Blood and Grey;
And in that welter of living fire
Be-jewelled and robed to his heart's desire
Was born – young Day.

(1929)

Vikings

The crash of the turbulent sea is around us, about us, below;
The green ice shimmers above us, as we steer through the
jet-back floe;
The sun is a blood-red disc that reddens a Polar sea –
And the Viking men are abroad again,
Bending the stout pine-oars again,
Exploring the wonderful world again,
Questing an unknown sea.

The 'Winged-hats' nod to the rowing, their rugged faces scan
The ice-green land of perpetual snow, unknown to the ways of
man;
The oars dip deep in the brine, and the shields along the side
Clank, as the ship bursts for'ard again,
Bucking her nose in the Polar rain,
Cutting through unknown seas again,
Testing an unknown tide.

Proud, though torn, is her bellying sail, with the Crimson Eagle
thereon,
Proudly erect is the Dragon's head, though its colour had long
since gone;
But the ship is hardy and tough, and the men are hardy as she,
When their Viking ships are abroad again,
Daring the uttermost wrath of the main,
Exploring the wonderful earth again,
Daring the wonderful sea.

(c. 1932)

Coloured Money

I am too rich already, for my eyes
Mint gold, while my heart cries
'O cease!
Is there no rest from richness, and no peace
For me again?'
For gold is pain,
And the edged coins can smart,
And beauty's metal weighs upon the heart.

How can I spend this coinage when it floods
So ceaselessly between the lids,
And gluts my vaults with bright
Shillings of sharp delight
Whose every penny
Is coloured money?

Storm, harvest, flood or snow,
Over the generous country as I go
And gather helplessly,
New wealth from all I see
In every spendthrift thing –
O then I long to spring
Through the charged air, a wastrel, with not one
Farthing to weigh me down,
But hollow! foot to crown
To prance immune among vast alchemies,
To prance! and laugh! my heart and throat and eyes
Emptied of all
Their golden gall.

(March 1937)

If I Could See, Not Surfaces

If I could see, not surfaces,
But could express
What lies beneath the skin
Where the blood moves
In fruit or head or stone,
Then would I know the one
Essential
And my eyes
When dead
Would give the worm
No hollow food.

If I could hear
Beyond the noise of things
Those Happenings
That stir the seed of sound,
And know the springs
Of Eden flood the round
Chasms of my twin shells, and beat
Old water-hammers on the hidden drums,

Then would I know my music wells
From the hot earth, and comes
Astride the long sea-organ
Of man's ocean.

If I could feel
Beyond each slender
Movement of her head, that trails
A track of earthless clay
Through gloom,
The rhythm titanic
Whence the tender
Gesture drifted, like a feather
Fallen from the downy throat
Of some winged mother,
Desolately, to fail and flutter,
Falter, and die
In the rented room –
Then would I plunder splendour
At the womb.

If I could feel
My words of wax were struck
By the rare seal
Of crested truth,
Then would I give bold birth
To long
Rivers of song.

Where is that inexhaustible,
That secret genesis
Of Sound and Sight?
It is too close for me,
It lies
Unexcavated by these eyes
In the lost archives of my heart.

(April 1937)

24

Palais de Danse

Can you not see within that small
And callow head, a brightness far
From this dance hall?
Her evening-dress
Is splitting like the chrysalis,
And when she stirs
A caterpillar moves.

Can you not see through her twin panes
Of coloured glass
That dusky room within
Her house of powder'd clay?
O stranger, stay,
Do you not see
A barbarous glory?

Observe her, one of that bright million
Wherever the blood roars and the limbs sing:
Unknown to her
One foot is tap-tap-tapping on the floor:
Her neck supports a brittle
And thoughtless miracle
Deadened with chalky pollen.
A cigarette
Like a white stamen with a burning anther
Is drooping from the flower tropical
That has two petals
Of dead, wet scarlet.

The sons of swingtime with their feet tap-tapping
The hollow platform wait the millionth moment
When to let loose on us the tinsel tiger.
Arise the fag-end boys from the tin-tables,
And slide into the hollow of the rhythm.

The crimson jazz is bouncing on the boards!

Where is she now?
She glides,
She comes
With a small shiny man,
And rides
Into the marrow of the Congo drums.

(April 1937)

Rhondda Valley

Here, are the stiffen'd hills, here, the rich cargo
Congealed in the dark arteries,
Old veins
That hold Glamorgan's blood.
The midnight miner in the secret seams,
Limb, life, and bread.

Here, are the strong hands hard,
And furrow-palmed alike
With the grasped pick.
These are the men; they chance
Another existence
Alien
To the fresh seasons of the sun and moon,
And where no winds are blown.

In the portentous dark
For bread
They make their stake,
And gamble with the spark
Of the non-dead.
Their fear

Is of the seeping gas; they pin
Their faith in props, and wear
Their labour on the skin,
As soldiers home
From the hot battle come,
With red
On hands and head,
So they
Arise to the light
In grey.

Here, are the gentle women with black lashes,
And here the infant in the shoulder-shawl.
With every man his bright bird at the throat,
And every girl a mavis at her heart,
Under the hills of coal.
I see the weary mountain and the mine;
Here lies the doldrum army, stranded men,
Rusting the shovel.

Yet these are they that knew the cage at morning,
They trod the fiery dew-shine at the cock-crow,
Through the Welsh fields to pit-head, line, or level.
For them the glimmering evenings and the voices;
They ran their darling dogs across the valley;
The callow nights upon the gun-grey mountains;
The street-lamp singer and the easy laugh
Defied at sundown the consumptive's cough.

Remains no lure along the hill-rich river
Now that their hands hang loose with barren creases
That feel no pick, only the cigarette,
Pale substitute
For the once strenuous fingers.
The swarming stars gesticulate like torches
Across the vaulted coal-mine of the sky;
The virile sunlight's irony
Burns on the grey pit-head
Like a mouth toothless, and dead,
And the sleek greyhounds
Mock with their streaming speed
The feet
That root the pavements of the grievous street.

At every door a ghost; I saw them lean
With tightened belts and watch the sluggish tide,
Through the long hours at the riverside.
Their shoulders prop the lintel-posts at evening –

And then, I heard them sing,
And loose the Celtic bird that has no wing,
No body, eye, nor feather,
Only song,
That indestructible, that golden thing.

(c. April 1937)

Heaven Hires Me

Heaven hires me; and my payment is in those
White instants of repose
Between the seething of my brain's all-coloured
Flora of woes,
Fauna from hills unhallowed.
While guilt grows
Stronger as I grow older
And lose love –
How break the terrible girders of the grove?

Yet; heaven hires me, and my weakness is
Threaded with alchemies.
Great Fowl along the combers of the sky
Undulate on such wings as suck
Breath from the pockets of far cliffs, and prise
The rocks apart with draughts that clear the muck
Out of a sickened sky. Heaven hires me still –

Though I do spit upon the marble face
And carve my name upon a seraph's breast
To testify to my unclean disgrace
The guttersnipe of dreams. Along the west
White gods move slowly, and the golden scales
Upon their breastplates twinkle momently
Now here, now there along the rim of Wales.

Though I do squander a largesse of un-
-Uprooted glory, yet heaven hires me still.
Though I do darken hourly the sweet sun
Of love and ruth – yet, hell
And heaven, so conjoined do make me.

(c. April 1937)

The Metal Bird

Job's eagle skids the thin sky still,
Her shadow swarms the cold Welsh hill.
The hawk hangs like an unloos'd bomb
And fills the circular sky with doom.
To-day across the meadow
There runs another shadow
Cast by a grizzlier bird that swings
Her body like a scythe, nor beats her wings,
A bloodless bird, whose mother was a man;
A painted bird of steel – a skeleton
That sheers shrill-naked to the screaming bone,
And bears her sexless beauty to the town.
O hawk with naked eyes!
O bloody eagle circling the dark skies!
Our century has bred a newer beauty,
The metal bird from the cold factory.

(c. April 1937)

The Cocky Walkers

Grouped nightly at the cold, accepted wall,
Carved with a gaslight chisel the lean heads
Cry out unwittingly for Rembrandt's needle.
These are the flashy saplings whose domain
I cannot enter.
They burn at lip and finger the stuffed paper;
The trouser-pocket boys, the cocky walkers,
Sons of old mothers, with their hats askew
Hummock the shoulder to the little flower
That lights the palm into a nightmare land,
A bloody basin of the sterile moon,
That lights the face that sprouts the cigarette
Into a sudden passion of fierce colour.
Down the cold corridor of winter nights

I see a thousand groups that keep
The fag alight, at walls, and in the sharp
Stern corners of the street:
These are the sprigs; flash boys, uncaught,
Treading the reedy springboard of green days.
Theirs is a headiness for they
Have burned their lives up to the quarter-mark.
The days move by them and the chill nights hold them
In an old, unthought conspiracy for they
Tinkle upon tin feet that send no root.
I see them at the cold, accepted wall,
The trouser-pocket boys, the cocky walkers.

(30 April 1937)

Poplar

Rapier!
Split feather!
Green feather gleaming
In the dark weather!

Eager invader of air
Once I saw you
Torpedo the cumbersome clouds
With a sliver

Of terrible emerald!
Slim feather
Arrogant
In the dark weather.

(c. 1937)

These Eyes Have Noosed a Hundred Hills

These eyes have noosed a hundred hills,
A thousand pines, the earth and sky,
This vast invention leaps and fills
The tiny lenses of the eye.

(c. July / August 1937)

Mané Katz

Interminable, the Avenue Raspail:
A sweaty day of August, '37.
A Sunday like the end of all the world
When no-one knows or cares if hell or heaven

Or nothingness cries trump upon tomorrow –
We walked the dragging street to find the house
And borrow
An hour of a painter's nervous time.

The house was silent and the windows grimed –
There was no answer to the iron knocker –
At last upon a window-sill we climbed
And peered into a pirate's glutted locker –

Upon a shadow'd easel there upreared
A silent canvas with its breast on fire
While all around it silence grew…

(c. August 1937)

Two Seasons

How shrill the bright limbs cried through martin-time
When the light belly fainted and my drum
Struck the lost rhythm.
That was a phoenix-day for the sweet bones,
When the lit blood ran emerald through the veins
Of the white fathom.

But now I hold in me the earth's decay,
And cold ferns heave their shuddering fronds through clay
Of ominous breath.
Between my ribs slants the November rain,
And I can feel the moss of death again,
Dank, in my mouth.

(c. November 1937)

Autumn

The lit mosaic of the wood
Stayed me at the turn of the road
To stare
At Autumn standing there
In Joseph's coat; a tree
Golden, and bright, and free
For head; his feet
In the rich earth were set.
The wind
Was tugging blind
At the fierce rainbow rags, the tattered turban,
Under a fitful sun.
Ambushed by beauty,
I a new creature, stand in Ancient Day,
Waylaid
At the turn of the road
By trees that bleed
And fill my eyes with plunder!
Is there no climax then? No ripe-as-thunder
Gong
Sudden, and strong?
Nought to be done
But only stand and stare and travel on.

(c. autumn 1937)

The Crystal

Hold her delicately
For she may break
And shatter her beauty
And wake
The dead rose echo
In man's heart no more –
O never again!
Hold her before the last
And the final pain
Buries the sudden splinter.

Hold sure the darling life,
The fragile thing,
The trembling stone,
Thy glory.
Hold her delicately
This moment in your fingers
And at your throat
For the arm leads to the heart,
And the current strikes
Along the hidden wire.

O delicately
Hold now the shining thing
The one and only
Before the radiance die
Or the lustre gone;
Before she slips
Through nerveless fingers
And from bloodless lips,
And smash her crystals
On the stones of winter.

(c. winter 1937)

To Maeve

You walk unaware
Of the slender gazelle
That moves as you move
And is one with the limbs
That you have.

You live unaware
Of the faint, the unearthly
Echo of hooves
That throughout your white streams
Of clear clay that I love

Are in flight as you turn,
As you stand, as you move,
As you sleep, for the slender
Gazelle never rests
In your ivory grove.

(c. 1937)

Poem

Body and head and arms and throat and hands
And all of me moves now across the dew
Beneath the trees of dawn, to where there stands
Against the sunrise the white shell of you;
My far feet crush the pearls they're moving through.

My hand has touched your hand and leagues away
Five fingers join five fingers bloodlessly.
And are you here, against the rising day?
Your head and arms and throat and lips I see
But where are you? And I? Am I with me?

(c. 1937)

How Foreign to the Spirit's Early Beauty

How foreign to the spirit's early beauty –
And to the amoral integrity of the mind
And to all those whose curve of living is lovely
Are the tired creeds that can be so unkind.

There is a brotherhood among the kindly
Closer and defter and more integral
Than any brotherhood of aisle or coven
For love rang out before the chapel bell.

There is no intolerance and no bitterness
As between sects where the full-hearted are
And to pray for the rare-natured and to have pity
On those of alien faith whose eyes are clear

Is to be insolent, is to be ignorant,
Is to deny the god-head – is to withhold
The focal christ of love; is to renounce
The only selfless language in the world.

(c. 1937)

Sing I the Fickle, Fit-for-Nothing Fellows

Sing I the fickle, fit-for-nothing fellows
For I have known them and have heard the yell
That rattles round the base of laughter's pail.
The empty-pocket boys who take no quarter,
For whom no childhood sings, and no hereafter
Rustles tremendous wings.
Their hollow sail
Fills with a fitful blast
As down the sea
They skid, without a needle or a star
Their careless privateer,
Agog for a gold island
Or a war
With penny pirates on a silver sand.
Sing I the way they tilt the cocky hat,
The lightning tongue that spins a cigarette
Along a slit.
The loveless eye
Like a wet pebble through the tilted glass.
I think their forebears gave the Spaniard trouble,
And in the mêlée made a job of it
With bleedy cutlass.

(c. 1937)

El Greco

They spire titanic bodies into heaven,
Tall Saints enswathed in a tempestuous flare
Of twisting draperies that coil through air,
Of dye incredible, from rapture woven,
And heads set steeply skywards, brittle-carven
Against the coiling clouds in regions rare;
Their beauty, ice-like, shrills – and everywhere
A metal music sounds, cold spirit shriven.

So drives the acid nail of coloured pain
Into our vulnerable wood, earth-rooted,
And sends the red sap racing through the trees
Where slugged it lay, now spun with visions looted
From whining skies and cold Gethsemanes
Of hollow light, and all the wounds of Spain.

(January 1938)

Spring

The palmerworm
That haunts my blood
Has wakened
To the cuckoo shout,
And stirs within
The crimson flood
Responding to
The double note.

Spring has no blade
To let the bead
Out of the flesh
But the tough branch
She lances
And the sharp green blood

Wells from the wound
No man may stanch.

I am as ripe
For sap to burst
And cover me
With fruit and flower,
And singing birds,
For I am cursed
With the long cry
Of plethora.

(c. spring 1938)

Watch, Here and Now...

Watch here and now, the modern Cleopatra;
The Helen-of-the-moment stand or stir
To challenge the eternal pride of Troy
Or Egypt's blinding queen: Here, they employ
The selfsame secret that long dynasties
Of women, conscious of their throats and eyes
Have proved magnetic: Here, the silky stride
Dawdles from hip to heel, as greyhounds ride
In waves, when they have slowed the silver film
To drifting rhythms of another realm.

Watch here and now this moment's full façade;
From toe to tress they flaunt the season's pride
With a conscious self-assurance, and appear
With limbs made topical with that veneer
They dare not question. Glamorous façade!
Behind whose lovely walls the tameless blood
Runs primitive, whatever fashion dress
The hidden limbs of ancient nakedness.

Hail then, bright Tyrant for this room is now,
Because of you, and your strong wand, aglow
And swaying like a small and flowering sea
Reflecting the full moon of your decree!
For, watch! The lively, and the drab of soul
Are welded here, into one shimmering whole.
Here, on this carpet where your banner flies –
Hail Fashion! And your Birds of Paradise.

(c. September 1938)

Au Moulin Joyeux

September Crisis, 1938

Here with the bread
We tasted anguish; here
The wine was grief,
While dynasties
Swung from a thread.
Yet, while we stared
Blind at a shifting fulcrum,
While our loves
Loaded the bleedy scales
And when to laugh
Were mockery,
Here with their burning flags
Of pride unfurled,
All women raised bright goblets to the world.

(September 1938)

Van Gogh

Dead, the Dutch Icarus who plundered France
And left her fields the richer for our eyes.
Where writhes the cypress under burning skies,
Or where proud cornfields broke at his advance,
Now burns a beauty fiercer than the dance
Of primal blood that stamps at throat and thighs.
Pirate of sunlight! and the laden prize
Of coloured earth and fruit in summer trance
Where is your fever now? and your desire?
Withered beneath a sunflower's mockery,
A suicide you sleep with all forgotten.
And yet your voice has more than words for me
And shall cry on when I am dead and rotten
From quenchless canvases of twisted fire.

(c. 1938)

I, While the Gods Laugh, the World's Vortex Am

I, while the gods laugh, the world's vortex am;
Maelström of passions in that hidden sea
Whose waves of all-time lap the coasts of me,
And in small compass the dark waters cram.

Thoughts of too old a colour nurse my brain:
No fable grows with me; I am no figure
Of ancient echo. Callow, and more eager
Am I for the spring bubble, than the pain

Of autumn and the rhythms of old time.
Why then, in a new vessel should arise
Archaic beauty in a storm of sighs?
If I have age already, when is prime?

44

Yet tears were ever big in beauty's eyes.
Tears glisten on her wings, and over breasts
Of haunted stone, and where her forehead rests
Upon a granite palm the dank salt lies.

(c. 1939)

Epstein's Adam

I have seen this day
A shape that shall outlive our transient clay
And hold
A virile contour when the world
Renews its crust
With our decayed and horizontal dust.
When this our perilous
Bright blood and bone,
Our hectic inches and the singing tone
Of throats and fingers are for ever gone,
And our sons' sons shall have forgotten us,
This shape that I have seen shall journey on
Erect along the winding corridors
Of the future years –
A craving of cold stone! A vertical
Symbol of man's perpetual
Dumb cry for light
Among the tangled Edens of our night;
A flowering fact;
A towering dawn of alabaster, hack'd
Into the yearn of Adam. His flat face
Lies parallel to the eternal skies,
His chiselled chest
Swells like a straining sail that holds a tempest
Captive within the rigging of his ribs –
The angular
Stone pistons of his arms – the architecture
Of surging thighs, deliver
A power and a magnificence

As brooks no question; this tremendous stance
Be-damns the bloodless mocker with his smug
And petty vision. Epstein fought
His burning tyrant for the shape he sought
And emptied a stone splendour from his heart.
There is a breed at large who have forgotten
That it is sap that drives the frozen tree
Into an April spasm; that it is blood
That drives the man; and that eternity
Is glimpsed through passion in a sudden light
That blinds the fickle processes of thought,
Thus in my sight
From those charged rhythms, suddenly
Adam broke free
And surged into my darkness, and made bright
The spirit's deathless hankering
Within man's body, that proud, tortured thing.

(June / July 1939)

Burgled Beauty

I burgled beauty in the night,
I stole a white coin from the sky,
And hid it in my plund'rous eye –
The moon, incredible and bright.

I have it still, that rifled thing,
Through body, heart, and brain it shines,
Yet, richer than a million mines,
I cannot buy me anything!

(c. 1939)

September 1939

This is the year of Our Lord
One thousand and nine
Hundred years
And thirty-nine
Since the Blood was Wine
And the Flesh was broken like Bread.

And the men of the equal tread
Have come into their own
And their bayonets shine.
This is the year of Our Lord
One thousand and nine
Hundred years
And thirty-nine.

(September 1939)

We are the thoughtless people.

We Are the Haunted People

We are the haunted people.
We, who guess blindly at the seed
That flowers
Into the crimson caption,
Hazarding
The birth of that inflamed
Portentous placard that will lose its flavour
Within an hour,
The while the dark deeds move that gave the words
A bastard birth
And hour by hour
Bursts a new gentian flower
Of bitter savour.
We have no power… no power…
We are the haunted people,
We…
        The last loose tasselated fringe that flies
        Into the cold of aeons from a dark
        Dynastic gown.

(September 1939)

She Whose Body Was in Pain

She whose body was in pain
Never shall be grieved again
She who was so loved rests now
Gently in the chalk below.

Hallowed be this place where lies
Her body, as in Paradise
She walks with Thee, her strength restored –
And, bless the Ones she loved, O Lord.

(October 1939)

Now Are Gathering in the Skies

Now are gathering in the skies
Round the gates of Paradise
Those white angels who shall come
And gently bear her spirit home

They shall bear her spirit home
Gently bear her spirit home
Very tenderly they'll come
And bear her quenchless spirit home

(c. October 1939)

Where Skidded Only in the Upper Air

Where skidded only in the upper air,
Clawed, winged and beaked for carnage, the cock eagle;
Or spun aloft on eddying breezes, bare
To heaven's teeth, the death-kite at sheer angle
Sliced a blue solitude; or, black and regal,
Her shadow moving over endless, fair
White domes of cloud in regions sharp and rare,
Only the condor rode, half god, half devil,

Now, tiny and intent along the old
Maw of a probeless heaven, flies, its breast
Arching at earth, a new and bloodless bird,
Whose metal womb is heavy with a cold
Foetus of bombs unborn, that, ere they rest
In death will revel in a birth of blood.

(c. 1939)

The Boy

I grow less patient of my pleasures now.
The fag tastes bitter by the fireside.
I walked the embankment on a night of snow
And found a huddled boy whose eyes had died.

All else cried youth from his cold capless head
Save only where his eyes were stabbed like wounds,
For at his brows the dryad bones I read,
And through his limbs lay caged the frozen hounds.

I saw him pattern'd pale: the midnight river,
His curtain, speckled with the swarming snow
Drawn up behind him. There he stands for ever
In me, unless into some stone I grow –

And do forget his eyes like broken glass –
The shattered panes of a deserted house.

(c. 1939)

The World

Blood on my skin, that, soon as the rains cool me
And wash away the colour, spreads again
Over my whirling body, bitter and warm –

When will these antish men that swarm my sides,
Invade my lost and secret valleys, know
How hotly burns their blood on breast and brow?

(c. 1939)

The Women of the World Inhabit Her

The women of the world inhabit her –
All women haunt the markets of her heart –
As, in a chip of quartz, the coloured veins
Proclaim an age of stone in miniature.

She is not only she – her eyes are aged
With woman-lore – her lips have sung a million
Gold cradle-songs, although a virgin child –
Her throat has filled an aeon with white bullion.

(c. 1939)

O Heart-Beats

O heart-beats – you are rattling dice –
My rattling dice
Proclaim the edge of precipice
At whose hid boulders stands a soundless sea –
These dice
Endanger me,
And spice
My days with hazards of futurity.

(c. 1939)

Sensitive Head

Sensitive head. And mouth
Big and untrembling
Now…
Great forehead, and
Eyes sunken, and fine
But vacant, unfocused
Now…
O God!
I know not
Who you are
Man, at the café
Table, but
Your life you have
As I have my life, we
Both tread the wire –
And you
Have stopped my heart
With love.

(c. 1939)

53

The Sands Were Frosty When the Soul Appeared

The sands were frosty when the soul appeared
From the tall shadows of the cliffs. The shells
Were aching with cold water. It was winter
Upon an island like a frozen beast
With grounded chin beneath an iron sea,
And hummock back of ink against the clouds –

(c. 1939)

I Could Sit Here an Age-Long of Green Light

I could sit here an age-long of green light
And count the trophies of the fruit, and bright
Emblems of flower – the coloured grasses growing
With long tufts blowing
And cones beneath their mothers' swarthy height.

I could sit here and catalogue a score
Of perfect coloured things before the hour
Had run its first rich minute. Here
Below me there
Are seven pebbles glittering, and four

Anemones burn out their tiny lives
Between the pebbles. Here, a beetle thrives
In the sweet air beside my shoe that breaks
The peerless pattern that a snowdrop makes
Untaught, and here an army of thin knives,

The grasses, menace a soft flower to tears –
And Lord, across the world, across the years,
The snowy clouds are drifting, see!
And all for me,
All for these eyes, these eyes my plunderers.

(c. 1939)

Dreams

Dreams
He believed in,
All
False dreams
This epoch scorns.
Climbed
The dim stair
No sane man dare
To climb.
He did desire
The moon's fire
That has no warmth for us this grievous time.
Alone
And rapt
He trod
The shadowy flight
Of chosen stone
That stirred
In a hollow light –
The moon
Was fever in his bone
While Europe clamoured for a gun-grey bird.

The worth
Of a lost globe enhaunted, and whose birth
Sprang from the parent heart, his crimson star?
Who knows?
I only gaze
Bewitched upon that ghosted moon he chose
My sight
Drugged with his lonely height.

(c. 1939)

Where Got I These Two Eyes that Plunder Storm

Where got I these two eyes that plunder storm
And gather tempests to the tiny lens?
Where got I lips that press the sunlight warm –
And taste the sinewy air, blown from salt seas?
These marvels, for the probings of the worm,
When the strong current cease?

Am I alone, or am I part of you
O world, O universe, O hidden, hidden God?

Voice
Sea sands are streaming, and the runnels rise
And the vast clouds beat wings along dark skies –
In rock, in flower and in the dank seaweed
Struggles the seed.
Do you not hear? The peevish gulls are crying.

(c. 1939)

I, Like an Insect on the Stainéd Glass

I, like an insect on the stainéd glass
Of some rich window – wallowing in its light –
Am sucked into the sunset, where the brass
Bright trumpets of the cloud blare for the night.

(c. 1939)

Swung through Dead Aeons

Swung through dead aeons, naked to the void,
Naked to sun and moon, and to those stars
Whose bright battalions march through streets of space
And break the brain…
Bare to God's anger and the ghosts of Time,
Nude for this love
The little World
Spun in a fevered dream;
Spun body, through an echo, lost, alone,
Through night and day, twisting
With that young cross

Swung at the axis.
I see you now that my quick fires are banked
At the skull's grate,
And at my heart, and the heat
Is in my hand.
I see you like a shuddering marble swung
In ceaseless circles from my burning palm's
Five pointed star;
But the bright hand
Leads Depthwards to the heart
That no man knows
And where lost legions are.

(c. 1939)

Autumn

There is a surge of stillness bred
In autumn woods of black and red
And in the stillness is the speed
Of satyrs; and the river reed
Sends a chill music into me
From every black and scarlet tree.

A stillness... the shrill music fleet
Escapes my ear, but *knocks* my heart.
O like a cloud suspended here
In gorgeous skies of death, the air
Of these rich woods emblazon me
With colours from a smouldering sky.
Then leaps my heart to the bone gate,
And at the gate the baffled heart
Knocks impotent for space, and cries
To wing the deep October skies –
My arms are branches! for they strain
Into the clouds of leaf; the rain
Falls softly now upon an age
Of black autumnal foliage –
O now the cave-cold breath through me
Blows dank from every forest tree,
And suddenly my soul floats free,
And lo! I am a crimson tree.

(c. 1939)

Eagle

Sheers the cock eagle
That is Satan's angel
Half god, half devil
Pinioned for plunder.

(c. 1939)

The Sap of Sorrow Mounts This Rootless Tree

The sap of sorrow mounts this rootless tree
When under earth the autumn sap should lie –
Yet no buds burst along the arms of me –
No leaves spring green from whence bright birds may cry –

My fingers like cold twigs unfoliaged
Stretch impotent for blossom, and my breast
Aches under pallid bark to be assuaged
With fruit and flower and to burn at rest.

(c. 1939)

Moon

Eternity in your sheer head
Ghastly, sharp, yellow moon, as dead
As death, tonight you frightened me
When your cold radiance brightened me,

Upon cold grass that showed my shade
By your grim light, and sharp, it made
Me feel the world below me shrink,
And I stood naked on the brink

Of Age! if men have fêted you!
I know that night I hated you.

(c. 1939)

No Creed Shall Bind Me to a Sapless Bole

No creed shall bind me to a sapless bole –
Dig I for the dark roots beneath the soil.
No foliaged candle and no aureole
Shall lure me from my toil
And snare my soul
When I stand fighting the Cathedral,
And the voluptuous clouds of Catholic
Narcotic ritual
And all the sick
And opalescent glory of the pearl
That do not stir
My spirit's eyes (to see Him standing there,
The spleenful Carpenter),

Shall be to feed my senses, not my soul
Which I would keep deliberate and whole,
Hard and unfingered of the sugar-smear.

Why the gold symbol when the man of flesh
Walked as we walk the evening's iron hush?
O I can see the whipcord Jesus slash
The men of cash
And fighting for his faith, the Jewish man,
How far from pomp, and plan!
O if the Faith were poor, we might have faith
In symbols and the knick-knacks of his Death.
The cross of splinters is more near to me
Than the jewelled Crucifix, the golden Tree –
There were no precious stones at Calvary.

(c. 1939)

As Over the Embankment

As over the embankment of the Thames
I leant at night, when sky and water
Urged one colour
Through the obedient eyes
While the gross head
Behind them seemed as dead –
I felt how my soul leaned into dark air
Over the cold embankment of my thought
While the dark night
Shut all the hundred truths away from me.

(c. 1939)

Blake

When I remember how his spirit throve
Amid dark city streets he did not see
Because his eyes were veiled with poetry
And at his heart the Prophet's wings were wove,

When I recall the squalor of his days
And then remember what rare fire was spent
When amid quenchless words he died, I praise
Whatever Gods were his, in wonderment.

(c. 1939)

Fame Is My Tawdry Goal

Fame is my tawdry goal, and I despise
My heart for harbouring that crimson yearning –
For well I know that it will bring no burning

Beauty before the windows of my eyes
For I, unknown, am spun with mysteries
And all the firmament of stars, my awning –
And yet I have a love for parrot cries

And cry o' nights for fame, that spangled thing
And only on grey evening of clear thought
I know that there is nothing sold or bought
That alters with the selling or the buying –
Yet now when I am painting, or am trying
To launch a frigate line of cargo'd thought
The foul red lips of Fame begin to sing.

(c. 1939)

Often, in the Evenings

Often, in the evenings, when I am alone, I think of death, and a
                                        terror comes over me:
It is not of the actual dying that I am afraid, although I have
                                        sweated with fear at the thought of it
But rather of the things I will never be able to see again, and the
                                        voices I will never hear any more.

(c. 1939)

I Am Almost Drunken

I am almost drunken with an arrogant
Madness of desire to follow in the line
Of England's poets who have raised high shoulders
Over the crowd, and cried mysterious words
Of deep and coloured music.
I am almost drunken with a wild
Longing to tread the burning line
Where the impetuous feet of those who yearned
For beauty with hot groan, have trod;
Whose eyes
Have in the grass-blade seen immensities
Of emerald light, and in the beggar child
The tragic splendour of a ragged wild.

(c. 1939)

Balance

In crazy balance at the edge of Time
Our spent days turn to cloud behind today –
And all tomorrow is a prophet's dream –
This moment only rages endlessly
And prime
Is always the long moment of decay.

(c. 1939)

The Torch

Over me the midnight elm
Loomed enormous as a hill
When from my torch I shot a stream
Of livid light, and in a beam
Of beauty the gigantic tree
Flared into ghostly tracery –
A spectre – naked, intricate –
A desolation of strange light
That spread through heaven, stark and rare
And coldness there,
And flames – I quelled
My torch's fire, and midnight welled
Into the attar of the tree
And a vast monster shadow'd me
Again –
O science gave me beauty then...

(c. 1939)

Stand with Me

1

Stand with me
Stock-still
As the lock-jaw
Rock,
And observe her flowing ever the loquacious river.

2

We have no
Dock leaf
For the sharp
Nettle shock

66

And the poisoned roots
Of grief
By the silver
Coloured water
Of the world
And of the Way –
O watch, today
The tide, with me, the silver-grey, of the ironic river.

(c. 1939)

I Sing a Hatred of the Black Machine

I sing a hatred of the black machine
Bred out of lust for the most loathsome whore
That universal man is constant to
And loves in blindness, setting her on high
Though she can break him at a whim, and toss
Him down her hollow sides that he has climbed
To reach the stagnant gold that gilds her lids
The silver powder of her rootless hair
And that red, cruel mouth that he has carved
To worship as the fountainhead of Life,
And truth and joy, but hidden crimsonly
Are set the jagged teeth of rotten bone,
The poison and the grief.
He has forgotten that it was a whore
He built to be his paragon, and now
Laughs at all gentle gods of love and sneers
At holiness and every thought that turns
To beauty that is neither bought nor sold
But burns her body silently, alone.
And for this harlot whose gross limbs spread wide
Over the world that heaves her natural body
Through space and time, these men have builded them
Black altars for her pleasure, factories
With loud unholy tongues and poisoned breath,
That point polluted fingers, black and grim

At a defenceless heaven, accusingly.
Caught in these clanky fortresses of greed,
Swung at a man-made axis, dizzily
Until the dizziness becomes a life
Within itself where the fresh air is lost,
And lost with it the healthy soul of man
And all the splendour of a million dawns,
Is whirled the hollow husk of man, the shell,
Who once indulged strong limbs among white flowers
And plucked an apple from the leaning bough
Or laboured at a work he loved, and bore
His triumph home in sweet fatigue and glee
With passion in his eyes, and shining limbs.
Money, to build machines to breed more money
To build a vaster horror that can grind
Metallic heels among the woods of dawn,
And guillotine the tender headed trees.
Money, to build machines to breed more money
To build a vaster creature that can suck
A hundred thousand men into its maw
And batter every heart into a cube
That gazes blind at fancy's curving flight
And the high spires of thought.

(c. 1939)

Lit, Every Stage

Lit, every stage of all the trillion
Chameleon stages that by night, by day,
Burst with inwoven, intermittent life,
With a trillion various lights, from daylight's rude
White sun, to the dark rented room below
Street level, where the tallow dribbles down
The bottle's neck: lit variously
For every minute of the marching day,
These stages that with overlap enshroud
The twisting world, with drama various

As it is real, tragic, gay, profound.
The murdered body rises in the pond
By starlight, while the men are playing bridge
Three stage streets off upon the second floor
Under a different light.
The harlot minces in the lurid air
And farmers knock their pipes upon the hearth
In houses by the twisting Arun river
Lit by a different light. The vagrants hunch
Their vulture shoulders in the dankest doorway,
And sleep upright, while over the black bridge
Rattles the twelve-eleven to Waterloo.
A minute, or a second, and the scene
Of million stages shift their props, and find
New wings around a million other sets;
For ever and for ever twists this world,
Of stages builded by the lives of men.

(c. 1939)

She Does Not Know

She does not know, but as she turns
Her oval head into the light –
She cries to Raphael and yearns
For plunder at his pencil point.

She does not know, but as she lies
In half light on the dark divan
Her bosom carved with candle flame
That Holland had a miller's son.

(c. 1939)

Life Beat Another Rhythm

Life beat another rhythm on that island
As old as her own birth.
We were the island people, and the earth
Sea, sky, and love, were Sark, and Sark, the earth
While round us moved the swarming of the sea.

(c. 1939)

Oh Sprightly and Lightly

Oh sprightly and lightly the Spring cometh nightly
With zephyrs of moonshine and ghosts in the blossom.
    Searchlights prod thin
    Fingers through
    Night's screen.

Oh darkness and sweetness of haytime and harvest
O warm summer stillness and the scent of her bosom.
    Stiff still shafts flood
    Dim clouds –
    Other mood.

(c. 1939)

What Is That against the Sky?

HEART

> What is that against the sky,
> Saffron coloured, huge and lonely?

MIND

> Peace my heart, for it is only
> The cold moon.

HEART

> Ah, she is so huge tonight!
> Huge and saffron, and so lonely,
> Naked and bright.

MIND

> Peace, my heart, it is the cold moon only.

(c. 1939)

Oh I Must End This War within My Heart

Oh I must end this war within my heart
This civil war and I the battleground –
But who to cry the truce? To wrench apart
The gory bayonets that give the wound?
And who can calm me when the bugles sound –

(c. 1939)

Beauty, What Are You?

I

Beauty, what are you
If sin and destruction
And arrogance please you?
Beauty, thou Pagan
Thou cold, other element,
Dead to our values.

II

The blood on the bayonet
The eyes of the harlot
The colour of nightshade.
The murderous army
Unleashed to the rapine
Is dark on the skyline.

III

Sweep through my day
With your hammering surges
Untainted by creed,
Terrible, sheer,
Omnipresent, unfailing
God whom I need.

(c. 1939)

The Modelles

In this, the vast absorption, burns the angel.
Strange among rowdy gods, that break the air
Of Now, with treacherous eyes and bloody hair
Is clay, his medium, his miracle

Of plastic birth, his lover, his white devil,
His world of silver flesh; the one his hands
Nurture in silence while the tocsin sounds
And Europe loads the gun-gray bird for evil.

(c. 1939)

I Found Myself Walking

I found myself walking on the world's wide and extraordinary
surface,
Scene of love, scene of battles, scene of a million irrelevances,
And all the small-talk of interminable and immemorial gestures,
I found myself suddenly walking upon this surface of a planet
Prehistoric, historic, terrible
A globe of many weathers, and for all that it is the Earth,
Unearthly.

Was I upon a moor, or among cornfields,
Was I leaning into a wild wind for foothold,
Was I among the barrows of the chalk downs
That I felt frightened by so being upon the historical surface
Of this earth, this immemorial world?

(c. 1939)

Along with Everything Else

Along with everything else, when the hovering war
Falls from the sky, and my door
Is filled and darkened by the insolent figure
With the crook'd forefinger –
Along with everything else on that day
I shall say to my visions 'goodbye',
And be taken away
Into the nightmare land of idiocy.
It was yesterday, beneath the accusing trees
I lay in the spring sun. A timid breeze
Stirred a dry leaf from last year's autumn dead
And it sounded like machine guns in my head
So loud it rustled in the silent air.

(c. 1939)

Am I to Say Goodbye to Trees and Leaves?

Am I to say goodbye to trees and leaves
And summer on the burning breasts of sheaves
That I have pondered by?
Am I to say goodbye
And hurry through a country I have loved
And bid farewell to the fields of season grooved
For the summer corn
And villages that watch the sun go down
With eyes of gold
And to the bold
Blunt shapes that haystacks make against the sky?
I do not know if I should say goodbye. .
No! why until the day comes, say goodbye?
But then, how many beauties would slip by
Without my seeing them again?
The sun may shine that day, and the white rain
Be absent.

(c. 1939)

To All Things Solid as to All Things Flat

To all things solid as to all things flat
He raised his little peacock-coloured hat

To all things lucent as to all things dense
He bowed his little head in deference

To all things coloured as to things of grey
He turned and smiled in a most gentle way

But ah, at all things white… at all things white
He could but stand and stare in grief's delight.

White wonderment upon him and within
That filled him to his cold and wrinkled skin.

That was his hour, his phoenix hour, his world
When all his flags of beauty were unfurled

Inhuman ecstasy of chill delight
Unworldly, lonely agony of white;

The white flower in the field, the white mane blowing
The white cloud over the white waters flowing

All things of white transported him to where
Long wings of crystal beat on stainless air

(c. 1939)

When God Had Pared His Fingernails

When God had pared his fingernails
He found that only nine
Lay on that golden tablet
Where the silver curves recline

When they have left his hands of cloud
And gleam in one long line.

'Rebellion!' cried the Angels. 'Where
Has flown the Nail of Sin?'
I saw it running through cold skies
Last night; so fierce and thin,
A silver sickle shape, that ran,
And ran – it was the moon.

(c. 1939)

For All Your Deadly Implications

For all your deadly implications I cannot restrain my delight
At your silver and silky rotundity, porpoise alight
In the morning sun, fat streamlined fish of the sky

(c. 1939)

O She Has Walked All Lands There Are

O she has walked all lands there are
In search of all things white –
For they are to her eyes a fair
And lonely sight.
But O, to her, beyond compare,
In all things of delight
Is the whiteness in the darkness
Of wanderers at night.

(c. 1939)

Grottoed beneath Your Ribs Our Babe Lay Thriving

I

Grottoed beneath your ribs our babe lay thriving
On the wild saps of Eden's midnight garden,
When qualms of love set fire the nine-month burden,
And there were phantoms in the cumulous sky,
And one green meteor with a flickering
Trail that stayed always yet was always moving;
O alchemy!
The fire-boy knocking at the osseous belfry
Where thuds the double-throated chord of loving.

II

Grottoed beneath your ribs, our babe no more
May hear the tolling of your sultry gong
Above him where the echoes throb and throng
Among the breathing rafters of sweet bone;
No longer coiled in gloom, the tireless core
And fount of his faint heart-beat fled,
He lies alone
With air and time about him and the drone
Of space for his immeasurable bed.

III

Grottoed beneath your ribs no longer, he,
Like madagascar broken from its mother,
Must feel the tides divide an africa
Of love from his clay island, that the sighs
Of the seas encircle with chill ancientry;
And though your ruthful breast allays his cries,
How vulnerable
He is when you release him, and how terrible
Is that wild strait which separates your bodies.

IV

Grottoed no longer, babe, the brilliant daybreak
Flares heavenward in a swathe of diamond light.
Stretch your small wrinkled limbs in shrill delight!
Gulp at the white tides of the globe, and scream
'I am!' O little island, sleep or wake,
What though the darkening gusts divide your mother's
Rich continent
From all you are, yet there's a sacrament
Of more than marl shall make you one another's.

(c. January 1940)

In the Fabric of This Love

In the fabric of this love
I hold for you are lions wove,
Are eagles, and a dew-drenched lamb
Shuddering in the dawn's first beam.

In my fabric England mourns
And all I know that's lovely burns –
Never turn the arras over
Where the ghouls are, little lover!

(May 1940)

May 1940

April gone by; the next faint fable-month
Is on us, rare, ungraspable, an echo
Of other maytimes when the thought was single
And the green hesitation of the leaf
Was prophecy for richness with no hint
Of darkened hours, and of being parted.

If not within the slow limbs of that oak tree,
If not within the uplands and the furrow,
Where has lost sanity a resting place
These days? for she has left those habitations
Built in God's image.

Be proud, slow trees. Be glad you stones and birds,
And you brown Arun river and all things
That thrive in silence through these hours of maytime –
Be glad you are not fashioned in God's image.

(May 1940)

Troop Train

The wheels turn over
And you are gone
O my little lover,
My only one.

Beneath my ribs are the spaces
Of the Pleiades,
And a blind ocean presses
Behind my eyes.

(c. July 1940)

Perke.
1940.

Fort Darland

Are there still men who move with silent feet?
And droop their thoughtful heads to earth, their hands
Listless along their sides? And are there lands
Where men are quiet in the way they meet?

The limbs my mother bore me know the wrench
That shapes them to the square machine of war.
My feet smash gravel and my hands abhor
The butt-plate of the rifle that I clench.

If my head droops, or my hands are not forced
Into my sides at the exact parade
Upon the asphalt square where men are made,
I am insulting England and am cursed.

As I stand motionless to-day and study
The red neck of the khaki man I cover
I shall not move but shall defy my body
By dreaming of pale gods that laze in ether.

(August/September 1940)

In the Lion's Yellow Eyes

In the lion's yellow eyes
Floats the grief of dynasties
Floats the pain of Emperors
Dying under tragic stars.
In the lion's eyes I see
The yellow lake of prophecy;
While the fickle gods of war
Tell me what I'm needed for,
In the lion's eyes I read
Of what it is I am and need.

(October/November 1940)

81

Every Gesture Every Eyelid's

Every gesture every eyelid's
Softest movement, every turning
Of the head or hand and every
Accent that is born is dying
As it empties its fulfilment
In the instant of its making
On the air surcharged with moments.

Every gesture every eyelid's
Dimmest movement dies and crumbles
In that black unfathomed region
Of lost gestures of lost voices.

(October–December 1940)

Leave Train

To your loveliness I travel
Through a bronze and yellow land.
England burns away November –
Every bough is a lit marvel
Pointing with a sentient hand
To where you stand –
Loveliest ember of the autumn's amber.

(c. November 1940)

The Shapes

(*London*)

What are these shapes that stare where once strong houses
Rose with their sounding halls and rooms of breath?
No, not their skeletons for those have fallen
Dragging to earth
The coloured muscles from a thousand walls,
And all the slow
Articulate organs that are now
The rubble that a cold well of the night
Erects its height
Of re-assembled emptiness upon.

What are these shapes that rise so chill and flat?
These shapes with pieces torn out of their sides?
Jagged from sky to pavement, laying bare
The secrets of a sliced blue nursery
Where painted jungles flake; or some grey room
Of dismal history that only now
Holds traffic with the day. Behind each other
Rank behind rank their wounded faces stare
In silent profile though their skulls have gone.
Like squares of vast and rotten cardboard ripped
Into these contours stiller than the brain
Of him who tore them ever could conceive,
They stare and stare.

They are the walls of skin, the skin of brick,
The brick that warded off the sun and moon;
Yet still the ceaseless elements attack them
Though what they guarded from the wind is gone.
The winds can circle now where blood ran warm,
And where the heart once stood the cold mist hovers,
Or gusts that whirl about each vacant womb
In whistling spirals, carry through the darkness
In fitful flight, torn papers that, bespattered,
Flutter their hollow wings.

What of this skin that only yesterday
Enveloped some far architect's bright boxes?
The coloured boxes that beyond black blinds,
Suffused with their especial emanations,
Were each a ranging world in microcosm,
The tinted projects and the memories,
The tear of sweetness and the blood of anger.

What of this skin that once enclosed all this?
Oh it will fall to darkness, to cold darkness
For it is ichabod and Life had fallen
Down into darkness through its quickened crate,
And it will fall to darkness, to cold darkness
Where nothing stirs among the dynasties.
The rubble that is rotting in the rain
Exhales the death of Warsaw and Pompeii,
Guernica, Troy and Coventry – all cities,
And every breathing building that died burning.

The shapes departing and the brick returning.

(November/December 1940)

To a Scarecrow Gunner

The Fates have willed it that you're living now
And not when Dickens might have watched your face
Your pigeon body and the tousled crow
That on your scalp finds perilous nesting space
And they have willed that Dickens cannot hear
Your sad inconsequent ejaculations
In such a curlew voice, as none may share
The portent of, save in hallucinations.

But so much less do I respect the Fates.

The Fates have willed the always insecure
And muddy forage cap on your dark head
Should not be part of Dickens' stock and store –
But now sits cocky while the man is dead

Who might have seen what's lost upon your mates.

(December 1940–February 1941)

From the Hot Chaos of the Many Habitations

From the hot chaos of the many habitations
From the urban wilderness
I have come at last
To these the wide highways
Of a green metropolis
An architecture as cool as water
A town of apples

(December 1940–February 1941)

Rather than a Little Pain

Rather than a little pain, I would be thief
To the organ-chords of grief
That toll through me
With a burial glory.

Wherefore my searching dust
If not to breathe the Gust
Of every quarter
Before I scatter,

And to divine
The lit or hooded Ghost, and take for mine
The double pulse; so come
Forth from your midnight tomb

Cold grief,
I would be thief
Of you,
Until my bones breed hemlock through and through.

(c. 1940)

The Two Fraternities

In death's unfelt fraternity the cold
And horizontal dead bestrew the world.
And you and I must add our little quota
To the globe's veneer.

What is more ghastly than death's brotherhood?
This doomed, this fragile life, this pounding blood,
This hectic moment of fraternity,
This *you*... this *me*.

(c. 1940)

With People, So with Trees

With people, so with trees: where there are groups
Of either, men or trees, some will remain
Aloof while others cluster where one stoops
To breathe some dusky secret. Some complain

And some gesticulate and some are blind;
Some toss their heads above green towns; some freeze
For lack of love in copses of mankind;
Some laugh; some mourn; with people, so with trees.

(c. 1940)

Onetime My Notes Would Dance

Onetime my notes would dance to any theme.
They are not dancing now for nothing dances
When the heart stands rigid.

I had a reed but I have snapped its body
Across my brain. I danced; I had a fiddle

But since I heard all instruments together
Surge up a crimson spiral to the sunlight
I have smashed my fiddle.

What once I would have sung I now deny
For I have heard the organ chords of grief
Break loose and cry from war's dark orchestra.

Oh I have crushed my bright notes underfoot
Like crystals in the dust – and of all that's me
Only my tears move.

(c. 1940)

London, 1941

Half masonry, half pain; her head
From which the plaster breaks away
Like flesh from the rough bone, is turned
Upon a neck of stones; her eyes
Are lid-less windows of smashed glass,
Each star-shaped pupil
Giving upon a vault so vast
How can the head contain it?

The raw smoke
Is inter-wreathing through the jaggedness
Of her sky-broken panes, and mirror'd
Fires dance like madmen on the splinters.

All else is stillness save the dancing splinters
And the slow inter-wreathing of the smoke.

Her breasts are crumbling brick where the black ivy
Had clung like a fantastic child for succour
And now hangs draggled with long peels of paper,
Fire-crisp, fire-faded awnings of limp paper
Repeating still their ghosted leaf and lily.

Grass for her cold skin's hair, the grass of cities
Wilted and swaying on her plaster brow
From winds that stream along the streets of cities:

Across a world of sudden fear and firelight
She towers erect, the great stones at her throat,
Her rusted ribs like railings round her heart;
A figure of dry wounds – of winter wounds –
O mother of wounds; half masonry, half pain.

(c. February 1941)

The Sullen Accents Told of Doom

The sullen accents told of doom
Approaching through the April sky
And menacing our feckless home
Of projects and of memory

And all our various loves, and all
Our crazed and lonely friends who try
To fashion bright and timeless things
In the chilly shadow of war's wings.

(c. April 1941)

Before Man's Bravery I Bow My Head

Before man's bravery I bow my head:
More so when valour is unnatural
And fear, a bat between the shoulder-blades
Flaps its cold webs – but I am ill at ease
With propaganda glory, and the lies
Of statesmen and the lords of slippery trades.

The time has come for more than small decisions.
I have my battleground no less than nations:
I have great traitors in the populous clay.
I am, no less than Albion, at war –
For while she struggles I must force my way
Into a land where sharper outlines are.

O let me find a way of thought that cuts
An angry line dividing this from that
And scours the soft weeds that have me caught.

(May 1941)

The Spadesmen

There is no lack of light and singing limbs,
Of throats and ribs and all the naked gear
That holds the quick breath in; there is no fear
That these will fail them and dissolve like dreams,

Now that each grave is scooped, each cross is varnished;
The robes of purple from the factory
Hang from the branches of gethsemane –
The coffins gleam and all the brass is burnished.

They have supplied the judas and the flails:
The ten-a-minute barbed-wire crown-of-thorns
Are in construction and a million pawns
Are ear-marked for the fever and the nails.

They have prepared the swabs of vinegar,
Long tears for cheek-bones and a load of lime.
The spadesmen have been working overtime
To raise so high a mound of golgotha.

(c. July 1941)

The Craters

For them the city crater is the mocking
Shadow of that zoneless chasm their breasts
Are empty with – that no strong earth can fill,
That nothing fills save time's unfaithfulness
And the thick hours of unhappy sleep
Dragging across the wound the sullen blanket
That each remorseless morning plucks away.

Huge figments of their wounds in the struck cities
Mock them at every turn and taunt the hollow
World of their emptiness that yawns and opens
Into a firmament beneath their ribs
That knows no planets, but a few dead stars
That wander desolately through the darkness,
Crying with phantom tongue of what is heard,
Of where they live and what their cold names are.

The echoes of their hollow'd lives, the craters,
Yawn with less hunger to be filled again
Than breasts that gape where once arose on high
Love's lofty masonry of rooted towers,
Love's windows and triumphant battlements.

(c. autumn 1941)

They Move with Me, My War-Ghosts

They move with me, my war-ghosts, my rebeller
And my conceder through the lies of hoarding,
Through gardens and dark rooms of various colour
And over fields of fever;
I move them on the asphalt square at evening,
Across the rugs of pleasure and the boarding
Of rats' feet and the dust's voluptuous layer,
They beat
Their warring rhythms in the war-filled weather.

Too small a home they share:
An angel's and a centaur's body greet
Each other fiercely on the narrow stair.

Blood beckons to my hand;
I am
Split tree-wise inly from the zestless morning
To when the fatuous moon pursues
The daft
And obsolete ram.

Split tree-wise; but what alchemy enfolds them?
What potion binds them, they, my ill-assorted?
(Irreconcilable, an april angel
Dazing one half of me and that triumphant
Pagan of thoughtless hooves and violent laughter
Filling the other.) What surrounds and holds them?
Nothing but skin.
Only a list of muscles holds them in.

Have I no strong controller of these forces?
My brain is webbed like water with slow weeds,
These days I cannot trust it. Here within me
A civil war makes idiot of my paltry
Skull-circled arbiter.
The gold nostalgia of the summer sunlight
Is mockery.

I walk the streets on imitation legs
Culled from a diagram, my hands
Hang anatomically at my sides
Reaching mid-femur, while I hold above
This double cargo in a ship, half love,
And half, that rides
The self-same sea-groove with wild laugh
Across these fickle, these infested tides.

(c. 1941)

Had Each a Voice What Would His Fingers Cry

His fingers that were trained to bind
The shadows of his mind
To paper with slim lead
Grasp grimmer substance than a pencil's measure.

Not cedar but the trigger's steel
Is what they feel,
And in a longer barrel
Lead of as fleet an impulse waits the pressure.

His perjured fingers have no throats;
His wrist no source of sound supports;
His crook'd forefinger
Curls like a tongue, severed and voice-forsaken;

Had each a voice what would his fingers cry
But 'Treachery!'?
Until their shrill pipes echoing up the arms
Should find and force the tyrant brain to hearken.

(c. 1941)

What Is It Muffles the Ascending Moment?

What is it muffles the ascending moment,
Dulls the long whetted edge of now, and blunts
Within me the bright needle of each instant?

Reality that holds my brain at bay
When I lean forward mocks me, and my eyes
Are webbed against the omnipresent day.

What is it clouds the anguish of crushed limbs?
Through darkened glass I watch the mimes of death
Move stiffly on a stage that flares or dims.

What is it holds the senses back from knowing?
And the eyes from perceiving?
And the dazed brain from grieving?
That drugs the heart, and stays the tear from flowing?

(c. 1941)

I Am For Ever with Me

I am for ever with me; I am always
Companion to the ghost-man whom I nurture.
Down the long streets of midnight I am with me,
In summer arbours are we bound together.
Drifting through starlight on a bruise-blue harbour,
Or wounded raw with the bright stones of winter,
There I am with me, haunting me for ever,
My ghost-man, and my lover.

I am for ever with me: throat nor finger
Have our strange nearness; nor the hammers beating
At the rich foundry of the heart are closer,
Nor breath for all its surge, nor the lips meeting.
The two familiar hands, the cold twin eyes,
And the fantastic ribs, all foreign structure.
The brow's portentous bone and the skull's laughter.
Even the sighs
That shake us, shake a mould of alien nature.

Alone, we haunt alone, this temporal pillar:
This doomed, this transient flesh, these chemicals
Of pallid colour.

We are alone, the incompatibles
Who love, and hate, foster and fear each other.
The ghost-man and the man of startling armour.
The Gabriel-headed scorner
White like light!
And I
The plunger.

Arises now in me the pilferer
Of hollow goods, the sprig and the swashbuckler.
I find in me the boy of shoddy glamour
And violent laughter.
The penny pirate and his cheap adventure…
Stars! and the cocky feather!

Sudden, I rise
And rip away his cloak of crimson paper;
Smashing his wooden sword, his tinsel visor
I pluck the gaudy marbles from his eyes –
When lo! there is another
Where he had been, white Gabriel the Scorner.

No plaster cast, no imitation figure
Is he, nor replica
Of some snow-muscled marble.
He is the one eternal
And terrible original.
For a lit moment flares this miracle
In the clay prison –
In me the modern angel has arisen.

Alive, the million million, and the dead
Breathe from the furrow and the wooden table:
Gulped with the wine, broken with bread,
Arising through the green sheets of the stubble.
In fruit, in flower, springing invisible
The phantom dead who knew the double owner,
The ghost-man, and the fellow
Of obvious colour.

One of a million million, I. The sons
Of our sons' sons and all the unborn people.
For each the autumn grief and the spring bubble;
For each the eyelash and the vein of purple,

For everyone, the double man: the torture.
The struggle and the grim perpetual laughter.
For everyone his Gabriel and the Mocker,
The stillness, and the fountain, and the Master.

(c. 1941)

97

The Sounds

Across the ancient silence of the ear
Meandered the lost sounds as aimlessly
As those that down the aisles of desolate
And cold cathedrals wander when at midnight
A window lost in a high cliff of darkness
Is tapped by branches or the wings of birds
Brush at its leaded panes; or when a great
And gull-winged Bible in a sudden draught
Rustles its sacred pages and the naves
Whisper of how a midnight leaf of Amos
Is lifting in the darkness, or a gust
Rattles the sheets of Jonah; from a vase
On the high altar a dead frond falls swaying
Through a black fathom and the flagstones sigh
For a cold second – yet the summer light
Played on our faces, warmed the impersonal flesh
Of neck and wrist and on the dusty ground
Our short, dark shadows anchored us in sunshine.

Five roads converged and where they met it seemed
It was the very focal point of silence,
Though these five radii were not from worlds
Of hypothetic beauty, nor slid in
To the dead, crystal centre of a theory
Nor, though they met in an unearthly silence
Had they through any earthless logic slid
Like icy shafts or strings of lunar light;
Oh no, they were five roads of broken brick
That bred where they converged death's empty disc,
For grief can cut a circle as exact,
But deeper than the men of geometry
Could ever score in regions of no blood.

How fragile in the emptiness they seem.
I can recall a group of lonely sounds,
Of little sounds that died as they were born.

Nine persons stand beneath a lifeless building
Singing of Jesus; what nostalgia

That far, lit name evokes as for a moment
Companionless, it wanders through the sunshine.
Oh what can be more lonely as it fades
Through sunshine than the naked name of Jesus?
The empty air decays and hangs; the metal
Heel of a soldier's boot clinks in the same
Hollow of sterile space, and in the same
Hollow of sterile space an old man coughs;
His white beard prods it as he nods his head,
Prods up and down through space in sweet agreement
At what the woman on the box is saying.

A clock has emptied its steel throat of three
Boulders that roll slow globes of cold through sunshine,
And as they die the voice they had interred
In the doomed notes breaks free again and flows
Like water liberated from thick shadows
That brood beneath a tunnel of three arches.

Behind the group against an iron railing
Leans, like a figure from a Hogarth drawing,
A hunchbacked man, and as he strikes a match
The sound speaks gunfire in the sunny darkness.

High cliffs surrounding the warm void are staring
From lines of dead eye-sockets. There are caves
And gulleys where no summer waters flow
And gleam with fish or seaweeds pink and gold;
The walls are dry and no anemones
Cling to the bricks, and though the sun burns on
There is no radiance. Above
There is no moving cloud to prove the sky
Is not a lifeless ceiling of blue plaster
Dead as the cliffs of brick; dead as the sun;
Dead as the space through which the sounds meander;
Dead as the five converging roads that meet
Together as the focal point of silence.

(c. 1941)

The Colt

Arabia is in your eye
That stares defiance;
And in your brandished mane, and in
Your arrogant stance.

You arch your throat; all Barbary
Is there; your raised
Forefoot descends like lightning and
England is bruised.

(c. 1941)

The Burning Boy

The boy that stamps his 'teens away like flowers
Beneath impetuous feet, his lilies dying,
Entwined with nightshade and the dagger'd roses,
Finds in the death of days a fever growing,
Making a pain of April, a wild season
Of cries, of lurid, of imperious voices.
Earth with earth's passions close around him. Banners
Break like square sunsets that brook no escaping,
He is enslaved in youth's vermilion prison,
He is found naked on a crag of tumult;
The shudder that the earthquake sends for courier
He feels long hours before the spasm of earthquake
Shakes him, a sapling and the tremor leaves him
Empty of all things but the blood that climbed him.

He is the emerald toy and earth's bright plaything,
Compact of wonder, grief, and sudden laughter,
And now, his childhood buried, given over
To sickness and the insistent pangs that rack him;
The burning boy! Half freshness, and half heavy
With the enormous throbs of the first Garden!
The eagle whets her blood-red beak within him;
And at his eyes his Mother's hazel colour;
These days a nausea haunts him, and a passion
He may not quench, until his clouds break open
And give upon a sky of startling stars.

(c. 1941)

Is There No Love Can Link Us?

Is there no thread to bind us – I and he
Who is dying now, this instant as I write
And may be cold before this line's complete?

And is there no power to link us – I and she
Across whose body the loud roof is falling?

Or the child, whose blackening skin
Blossoms with hideous roses in the smoke?

Is there no love can link us – I and they?
Only this hectic moment? This fierce instant
Striking now
Its universal, its uneven blow?

There is no other link. Only this sliding
Second we share: this desperate edge of now.

(c. 1941)

Swan Arrogant

There rides within my heart swan arrogant
Beneath the muscled branches of thick thought
Holding my brain at bay. Each day
I wrench the boughs apart until
I can no longer hold them. From the well
Of my confusion the dead waters rise
In layers of silence widening my eyes
With nothingness. No swan; I cannot see her; only
The flat reflection of the branches latticed
Under the snags, the drifting water-weed
And rotting wood.
How can I lure her from my labyrinth
Of flesh and blood?

With the dank bread of grief? She will not come;
Nor for the metal notes that beat
Their frozen logic from my instrument.

Yet once, once only, very mistily
I saw her shadow through the floating leaves
And she is here; her body is in my heart,
Too close for me to see, save suddenly, with earthquake start
Shaking my foliage.
Show me myself! How impotent
I strain my spirit's sight! O slake
My eyes with beauty, see, the lake
Is dark with love; flare now, and flow
So that my eyes
May fill with whiteness as she comes again,
And rides, so naked! and so terrible!
And rears out of the driftwood of my brain.

(c. 1941)

London Buses

Each day their steep, blood-red abundance winding
Through corridors of broken stone is binding
The city's body with a living thread
That like a vessel weaving through grey flesh
Its crimson mesh
Of anger, surges onward like a tide
Among the empty ruins and the dead –
And those who have not died.

(1941)

104

A Reverie of Bone

1

I sometimes think about old tombs and weeds
That interwreathe among the bones of Kings
With cold and poisonous berry and black flower:
Or ruminate upon the skulls of steeds
Frailer than shells and on those luminous wings –
The shoulder blades of Princes of fled power,

2

Which now the unrecorded sandstorms grind
Into so wraith-like a translucency
Of tissue-thin and aqueous bone: I ponder
On sun-lit spines and in my reverie find
The arc-ribbed courser and his mount to be
Whiter than sexless lilies and how slender

3

The spleenful hands can turn: I see the gelid
Twigs of the brittle fingers lie so still –
And all the arctic filigree of feet:
The porcelain of the breastbone and the pallid
Ulna as downless as the lyric quill
Of some sky-wandering pinion that the sleet

4

And gusts have stripped of all its clinging hairs;
So that a sliver-shred of whiteness wanders
Across the stars until the night-winds fail.
O ribs of light! bright flight, yours are such stairs
As wail at midnight when the sand meanders
Through your cold rungs that sieve the desert gale.

5

O string the arrogant ribs with spider-twine
Torn from those webs that hold the murderous arms
Of thorn-crazed boughs together, that a gust
May pluck the resonant threads to a white rune
Of memory, a music of fled forms,
An immemorial cadence from the dust.

6

Bright lyre of ribs, cold cage of white tusks curling
Deliberately from the razed spine's pagoda
To right and left, a phalanx, tapering
To the basin'd pelvis and to where the skirling
And cave-cold winds within the skull are louder
Than were the pulse-drums at the temples leaping.

7

O you white blades and thin stems interlaced
And freed forever from the oppressive clay,
I watch you glimmer by the dying light
Of my dark brain, as, pranked across a waste
Of restless gloom, the sea-froth seems to stay
A moment frozen to an aqueous night.

8

A heaving sea-hill gulps these sudden chalk-
White markings, as a sand-hill drags the bone
Into as deep a maw, from hour to hour.
For dunes, the sustenance of the hollow stalk,
For waves the silver diet of the lone
And yet gregarious ghosthood of the flower.

9

Cold spectre-flower, that, dying, lifts a sister
To the insatiate surface of the ocean.
The buried stalk, less rapid through the dune
Is no less sure, for the dry heavings muster
The brittle brothers though with tardier motion
They climb their stifling stairways to the moon.

10

Between the spirit and the impending motion
Of rumoured weather the Lacuna kneels
Among the dunes, that, from the skyline's truce
To the numb centre of the desolation,
Heave their dry combers of blond shale no keels
May cleave until the ships of wind break loose.

11

There are no keels for this forgotten ocean,
Not one, for all this ochreous waste; no wave
Feels its hot forehead at the sudden turn
And pressure of a vagrant prow break open,
And there would be no foam of ruth to lave
The wounded comber if it were to happen.

12

These shipless, corrugated oceans cry
With the false voices of their surface rollers,
'We are a fathom shallow; we are breaking
Over a paddler's base,' and the pursed eye
Of the helmsman in a lidded language mutters,
'Here lie the shoals! Beware! The waves are flaking!'

13

Yet the impossible helmsman with his eye
Schooled to the pregnant by-play of great waters
Forgets waves of repetitive, stumbling shale
Can undulate as though a shelving bay
Lay by, and yet be deep as those cold quarters
Of flaccid ooze where all the strong lights fail...

14

Forgets that the misleading breakers are
Curled by the winds and that beneath them falls
Depth upon depth, down, down to the pulseless places.
And in a ship whose mast impales a star,
Whose sails drip glass along two skylines, calls
For vigilance, the while his free keel slices.

15

So are the deserts where they lie immured
Or on whose surfaces, from time to time
They congregate, the skeletons of those
Whose days of storm or rainbow death has cured
Of surfeit, whose rich, crumbling hours of prime
Are over, that were hot as mine and yours.

16

The plains remain. The sun; and the chill moon
With taunting freshness circles the old sky,
And the ancient winds for whom there's no decay.
Is every part of man to slide so soon
Into the namelessness? ah no, for see,
The bone remains and will not burn away.

17

How still it lies when the thick storm abates
And every grain has settled from the sky.
A lord upon a steed of alabaster
Rides on his side, until I ruminate
How, lost in the wild desert of the eye
A black horse stumbled northwards to disaster

18

Through endless sand; the throats of steed and rider
Coughed out their last before a waterless death –
Together lying, they are yet alone.
I glimpse them as they were, less rare, but prouder,
The bright blood coiled around them like a wreath
Of sultry vine that swarms their plinths of bone.

19

The sentient columns of imperial bone,
Charged with the stormy marrow, green with grief –
O desert rider, riding on and on
Across the hey-day of your glory, torn
Across the throat, across the breast, with life
As tameless as the tracts you trample on –

20

I see you Rider, my imagined Rider
In purple, and the great locks of your hair
Lift in the sunny wind; you cry and swing
The dancing courser upright – you were cruder
Than now, as chill and delicate, your bare
Twin femurs lie astride the scaffolding

21

Of that which sieves the softly pouring sands –
The sunlit arches of your horse's ribs
Are one with yours in that which is more rare
Than pride of carriage, or the grip of hands
Upon a lashing mane, and all the webs
Of veins that branch and throb from sole to hair.

22

O prince in purple you are lovelier now,
Your bracelets, curls and lips and eyelids gone,
Your studded crown, your quick, imperious breath,
Your heart that some gaunt eagle far ago
Carried aloft beneath a desert moon
To the matted eyrie of its ghastly kith.

23

O prince long perished you are lovelier dead,
Though when you died a bald and screaming brood
Tore at the broken engine of your breast
Upon a ledge above the drift and flood
Of many airs and though your warm, sweet blood
Once clogged the claws that gripped a crag's cold crest.

24

You are more lovely now: desireless
Your bones comply with every feckless wind
That shifts the pouring hills from place to place.
Freed from the tumult of the blood's excess,
And the insistent cloudland of the blind,
Slow, cumulus of flesh. The breast, the face,

25

The thigh and all the members choked your white
Reality, your stern, ancestral joy,
Changeless beneath the flux of tidal clay.
Your perfectness reflects the moon at night –
O bones of lords and mendicants, enjoy
Your fleshless journeys through the night and day.

26

What is more exquisite than to be free
Of all that presses on the crying core
Of the long bones, that now, so nakedly
Can hear the desert winds along the scree,
How vibrant! where they were so drugged before,
By the dumb bullion of the shrouding clay.

27

Queens in their tombs are mouthed by the furred lips
Of humid plants, or stretched upon stone shelves
Of granite, where the sandy sunlight fingers
Ruminatively with hazy fingertips
High tiers of skeletons, and skulls revolve
Among the motes where the dank lizard lingers.

28

For these, the pride of palaces, a tomb;
But for each bone that whitens in the dark
A million blossom on the desertlands.
The skulls of nomads echo in the gloom
To the lions' throated thunder or the bark
Of jackals as they scour the shadowy sands.

29

There is a pearl white arabesque of bones
Behind my eyes where the harsh brow encloses
These bones my visions conjure; I can see
Them lying pranked across a brow of stones.
Beyond them a dramatic mountain raises
High flanks of cold and silver-coloured scree.

30

And yet not only in the brain's grey spaces
Which, at the imagination's astral touch
Flare into focus, all horizons failing...
Not only through the wastes of thought uprises
A ghosted mountain lit by the full torch
Of a sailing moon that never ceases sailing...

31

Not only in the brain, nor in the heart
Nor out of love, nor through untethered fancy,
Is that cold mountain littered with the white
Residue of the dead, as though its bright
Steep sides were dusted with dry leprosy –
Nor any other death-engendered sight

32

Which I envisage in deserted places –
But, in the ruthless regions of what's true –
And I can only hope to grasp the worth
From vast and valid landscapes, while Time passes
Beneath my pen-nib as it trails the blue
Thread of my thought behind each glimpse of truth.

33

This is no figment but a spilth of all
That is so beautiful in the long dead –
Those delicate carvings that deny the night.
Over the burning scarp a prophet's skull
Revolves before the winds, its lengthened shade
Cruising before it as it rolls through sunlight.

34

All this is true; this hand that props my forehead
Is no more real than those hands of frost
That lie in myriads like an astral choir
Of endless gesture, eloquent though dead.
Hands yearning, voiceless through their quilts of dust,
O skulls, blades, ribs made white in the long sunfire.

35

O passionless, amoral, unearthly whiteness
Emptied of ardour like a thought of crystal
Scoring a circle in the air of Time:
Closer to darkness is this loveless lightness
Than to the wannest breath of colour. All
That is most ultimate and clear: the prime

36

And essence of a dream, that flowering, loses
Its colour-tinctured parts on finding climax
And consummation in a spectral land,
Vaster than arctic, rarer than where cruises
The frigate moon, is your demesne that works
Its magic in the thighbone on the sand.

37

What bears you on its surface? the blanched whale
Through floating towers of translucent ice
Carries your alchemy in undulations
Through sunless waters, and along the gale
Fly fragments of your chill unearthliness,
The gulls that scream above stark habitations.

38

As bleached and scrupulous as that stern linen
Da Vinci laid forever underneath
The isolation of the unfingered loaves,
The desolation of the untasted wine,
The thirteen double islands from the Earth,
Stiff, icebound and estranged from vines and sheaves,

39

Show with their pool and crust how pure is flax,
How cold it is and how immaculate
And close it is at the Supper, charged and lorn
To the asceticism of the stern stalk
Of hollow bone that the same master sought –
Blanched, holy whiteness that continues on.

40

And every dawn the scything sunlight sweeps
Upon the strewn mementos of the token
Epochs of passion; on the breastbone of
A suicide; or the rich vapour steeps
The jawbone of a merchant, or the broken
Rib of an alchemist protrudes above

41

A knoll that by the noonday shall have slid,
Under the wind's compulsion, to a vale,
And dragged the stringless bow sand-fathoms under,
And all is changed, the hills as hot as blood
Have given place to corrugated, pale
And ash-grey tracts that have thrown up fresh plunder

42

From the sterile torpor of the desert's womb;
So that across the desolate plains are littered
Fresh relics of incongruous dynarchies –
Bones, that when sunrise flowered through the gloom
Were sunless, glitter now, where they lie scattered,
Scudding across the melancholy land.

43

What of all this? – why should I harp upon
Ribs? when I have, it may be, thirty years
To go before my own come into their own…
That which is morbid in my brain and bone
Must out, for it is so with our long tears
Which, pouring, blunt dejection's direst thorn.

44

A reverie of bone the beautiful!
Science must strike its colours at the white
Articulate splendour, be it peace or war.
Enough of wonder and of death. Set sail
For other waters of translucent light
Where life and breath more vast and splendid are.

45

I sometimes think about old tombs and weeds
That interwreathe among the bones of Kings
With cold and poisonous berry and black flower:
Or ruminate upon the skulls of steeds
Frailer than shells and on those luminous wings –
The shoulder blades of Princes of fled power.

(c. 1941–2)

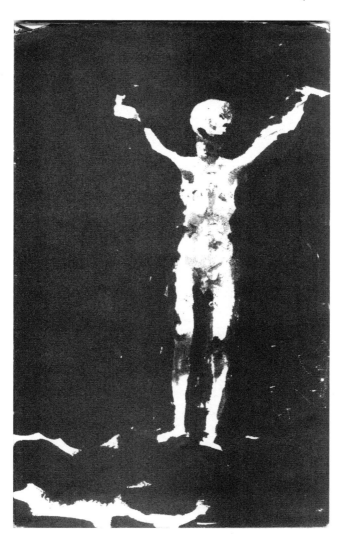

Suddenly, Walking along the Open Road

Suddenly, walking along the open road I felt afraid.
I saw the stars and the world below my feet
Become a planet, and I was no longer
In Wiltshire. I was standing
Upon the surface, the edge of a planet
That runs around the sun.
I was in danger.
For all the comfort of the elms, the banal
Normality of houses with their garages, the apparent
Changelessness of the ploughed field on my right –
All was in danger.
A marble spinning through the universe
Wears on its dizzy crust, men, houses, trees
That circle through cavernous aeons, and I was afraid.

(c. December 1941–March 1942)

They Loom Enormous

They loom enormous on the shrivelling beaches,
The Silent Horses.
Upon their gun-grey backs, like pallid carvings
Are the Ivory Men, whose eyes are torches
That burn through water.
There is no sound,
Though the huge hooves stamp the sand.

(c. December 1941–March 1942)

Maeve

If when I married you I was in love
As I imagined at the time I was,
Then what is this new Illness? and the cause
Of my heart crying from its midnight grove
Of ribs, for, trapped like an alizarine bird
In the heaving cradle of the bended boughs
It shakes anew its violent wings and grows
Maddened the moment that your voice is heard.

Either it was not love I felt before
Or else love climbs like fever. I hope it is
That I was *not* in love, for even This
May then grow wilder yet, though any more

Of love seems unimaginable; ah Maeve
I do not wish more glory than I have.

(January 1942)

What Can I Ever Offer You

What can I ever offer you that shall
Not be a mockery when I compare it
With this portentous proffering which your heart
Has throbbed above, so long, my cargo'd girl?

Beneath your heart the dynasties of clay,
Beneath your heart lie coiled the happy rivers,
Within the crouching babe the tears of lovers
Drip from the cheekbones of the night and day.

(c. March 1942)

O, This Estrangement Forms a Distance Vaster

O, this estrangement forms a distance vaster
Than great seas and great lands
Could lay between us, though in my hands
Yours lie, that are less your hands than the plaster
Casts of your hands. Your face, made in your likeness,
Floats like a ghost through its own clay from me,
Even from you – O it has left us, we
Are parted by a tract of thorn and water:
The bitter
Knowledge of failure damns us where we stand
Withdrawn, lonely, powerless, and
Hand in hand.

(c. March–April 1942)

An April Radiance of White Light Dances

An April radiance of white light dances
From the long silver pastures under Pendle,
Dances from grasses, glances
Among the uncurling leaves I'd fondle
Were my hands moth-soft, slight
And light as a petal:
But they are heavy bone and blood and clay
And are too clumsy for this faëry day
Of exquisite and shimmering
Foliage and tremulous wing.

Too coarse, my hands among the delicate marvels.
Too coarse my brain while the deft day unravels
Coiled april's foliate thread: too coarse my heart,
For as I tread the immaculate lakes of dew
I know it to be rotten as the lung
Of an old miner; yet, the pitman's throat
Cages the Cambrian thrush, and through
My turbid heart it may be I can fling
Across the face of war this song for you,
Of naked spring.

(c. April 1942)

May 1942

Now is the month of maying
While pretty lads are slaying
Each with his metal lass

(May 1942)

Blue as the Indigo and Fabulous Storm

Blue as the indigo and fabulous storm
Of a picture book long lost where islands burst
Out of the page, exploding palm on palm,
Are we, whom the authorities have dressed.
For we are bluer than the fabulous waters
That lap the inner skull-walls of a boy
So that his head is filled with brimming summer's
Dazzling rollers which make dull the day
Surrounding him, like an un-focused twilight,
Such waters as uplift a rippling acre
Of naked jelly through the sunfire drifting
With at its centre a vermilion ember
Across whose fire the transparent eyelids rove
O fiercer than the azure lights that flare
At the lit core of fantasy. We move –
See how the sick kingfishers take the air! –
In brilliance past the Southport pier
Yet we are shapeless in our azure suits
Which hang in monstrous folds. Around our throats
The twisted snakes of fire burn all day long,
And tenderness recoils from our preposterous boots.

(June–September 1942)

Curl Up in the Great Window Seat

Curl up in the great window seat, your heels
Beneath you in the cushions while you watch
The summer rain fall with unnatural darkness
Beyond the pane. Move your dim arm and touch

The glass that shields you from the violence
Of the primeval gods. Then turn your eyes
To the book upon your knees, and make pretence
To read, but do not see it. Then heave such sighs

As the melancholy drifts of water heave
As they draw back their salt drifts from a cove
Of clashing shingle – then, my darling, leave,
And suddenly, the room, and weep, my love.

(c. June/July 1942)

Digging a Trench I Found a Heart-Shaped Stone

Digging a trench I found a heart-shaped stone:
Freeing its surface of the loam, I held
It – why so tenderly? – in my grimed palm.

I let the army shovel fall away
And held the heavy, heart-shaped stone within
A cup I formed between my working hands –
As though it were a wounded bird whose breast
Throbbed delicately against my finger-tips.

And it grew heavier and heavier
Until it had become your heart and mine
Fused in a fierce embrace of solid stone.

(c. 1942)

121

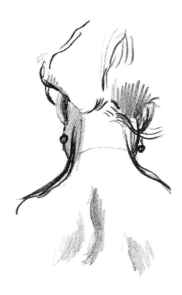

Absent from You Where Is There Corn and Wine?

I

Absent from you where is there corn and wine?
You have gone out of the leaves, out of the sunshine:
My spirit sickens and the air is brine-
Less.

II

Absent from you – absent from sight and sound –
Clouds are but clouds and the ground is only the ground;
Say you that birds yet sing? Or that the heart is bound-
Less?

III

A light has fled out of my bones and from life its rhyme.
Gulf'd in a failure of love I can hear the chime
Of childhood's bells, forlorn, as I wander time-
Less.

(c. 1942)

I Am the Slung Stone that No Target Has

I am the slung stone that no target has
Thirty two summers from the slinger's hand.
Not of my making is the speed
That flights me, never mine the deed
That sent me headlong.
O
Where do I go?
Where do I go –

Death, lust and fever as I fly
Flow through me, hideous ghouls; and saints
Wave wings like sheets
And as white
As Ahab's whale.

(c. 1942–3)

If I Would Stay What Men Call Sane

If I would stay what men call sane, then Lord
Save me from my Imagination's Truth –
Now, now, now, now, each now a bloody word
That speaks some simultaneous death

And yet, Lord, save me from a slurring brain
That cannot dare to realize, that now
Now, now, the bomb strikes, and flung limbs are strewn
Severed and fresh since this short poem started
In (who cares what poor country)

(1943)

Poem

Taller than life, deployed along the shallows,
Up to their ankles in the sluggish water
The skeletons, black egg-shells for their heads,
And full of air as pylons, stand,
Like charcoal-boughs. Upon
Their skulls sit birds whose droppings cake their shoulders
With luminous chalk. Behind the scaffolding
Of that which once rang to the senses' touch
Is darkness: all is darkness on the shore.
Only their entrails, brilliant as fresh flowers
Flame in their pelvic basins.

(c. 1943)

The Glassblowers

Turn of the head… turn of the hand… such wiseness in
These gestures of craft's ritual lies, and such
A lyric ease pervades their toil as makes
Their firelit bodies lordly as they blow.

Turn of the hand… turn of the head… such a rare tremor
Of skill that weaves and winds and coils along
The giant flute they fondle, spin, and give
Their hoarded breath to, in the raddled darkness.

There is a molten language that is glass
Unborn, a poetry of barbarous birth;
It sings in sand and roars in furnace-fire;
The blowers breathe it voiceless, as they pass
Through brimstone halls and girdered aisles of ire.

Here, in this theatre of fitful light,
The dancers cast their long and leaping shades,
Their heavy feet thud on the firelit stage,
For they are dancers of the arm and hand,
The finger-tips, the throat and weaving shoulders:

Between the head and feet a rhythm of clay,
A rhythm of breath is wheedling alchemy
From the warlock sand.

Their cheeks are blown like gourds that sweat and flush
With goblin hues, rose-gold, diaphanous,
The violet glow and the alizarine blush.

The air is full of gestures suddenly lit,
As suddenly withdrawn. The mammoth throats
Of arches, gulp the dancers, flame, and loom.
O factory fantastic! cave on cave
Of crumbling brick where shackled lions rave
And howl for gravel while their blinding manes
Shake radiance across the restless gloom.

It is the ballet of gold sweat. It is
The hidden ballet of the heavy feet
And flickering hands: the dance of men unconscious
Of dancing and the golden wizardries.
Rough clothed, rough headed, drenched with sweat, they are
As poised as floodlit acrobats in air,
They twist the throbbing fire-globes over water
And whirl the ripe chameleon pears, whose fire
Threatens to loll like a breast, or a tongue or a serpent,
Over the breath-rod and the surly trough.

He has withdrawn the fire-flute from the jaws
Of cruelty, has gathered at its tip
A lemon of ripe anger, has become
A juggler spinning fire, and when he puffs
The hollow rod, his hands are spinning still
As burgeons at its lip the dazzling fruit
That burned the lips of Adam, yet more fair
Than the bleediest apples of that Orchard were.

See, it is spinning through the shadowland
Shaped like a sphere or giant worm of flame,
A slug of light, a snake, or fruit of air
According to the wisdom of his hand.

O you have juggled with an Element
And tamed its heart – the sands and the flames are now
This delicate transparency that clings
To its last, fleeting tincture. Naked and white
It lies at last, snapped from the rod, among
Its delicate echoes on the factory floor,
And what was molten, tinkles; what was twisting
In dragon wrath is calm and twists no more.

(c. 1943)

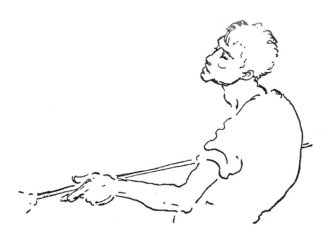

Dead Rat

Were I a farmer I would call you vermin
Because you'd be the villain of my crops
And gnaw my wealth, but I am not a farmer,
But only one that walks the farmers' fields,
And so when I came on your stiffen'd body
Lying alone and flowered with frost, your eyeballs
Glazed and your little front paws so beseeching
Crossed on your breast and pink like human fingers,
And when I saw your deadness in the frozen
Light of the winter morning, I, unmanly,
Unfarmerly, and most impractically
Felt that rats even have a right to live
And knew that there was beauty in your body
Dusted with starry marvels of bright frost,
And beauty in the little hands you crossed
Upon your breast before you died this morning.

(1944)

For Maeve

You are the maeve of me as this my arm
Is the joined arm of me; the heart within
Which I have heard so long yet never seen
Is thus – like these, you are my fount, my limb –
Yet more than these: you are the maeve of me.

Birthbed or deathbed, cradle and grave of me.
What is there that I lack? Yet what have I
More palpable than the immuring sky?
I can be lost in a familiar realm,
The more my knowledge the more lost to be
In all you are who are the maeve of me.

(c. 1944)

Tides

Always you are remote and islanded
In silences that so belie the ardent
Torrents that course beneath your gentle clay,
Whose sources you are unaware of, lady.

Yet of your heart-beat I have knowledge, lady,
For I have heard the drum-throbs momently
Quicken with mine and rap the fourfold thunder
Until from nod to footfall I am music.

You are the burden of my body's music;
My limbs are flutes and their strange timbre is
Engendered through my love of you, the lonely,
Remote and lunar mistress of my senses.

More of me cries for you than in my senses
Cries, for always a remoteness lingers
About you like a vestment of the moon,
O whitely, it is earthless; it is foreign.

I ruminate on this and still am foreign
To you, my island, though your subterranean
Rivers I understand, and your unbridled,
Intense and helpless love for what is lovely.

Your woodland pulse, your gestures, more than lovely
To me; your mirth, the tears you mix with mine
When great swans die, your limbs that with mine lie,
Your voice in the sunk hours, these are become

My daedal diet. Lady I become
Each day, each hour of this little journey
We make together less alone, although
You will be always far and islanded.

(c. 1944)

Because Last Night My Child Clung to My Neck

Because last night my child clung to my neck
He was not therefore mine.
Life's cycle spinning in a void of cold
Lay in between.

It was disparity, it was mutation, it was cold Lethe flowing.
What I held in my arms was a leaf, a bird, a little frog.
I have forgotten their language.

He was a loved one seen through a carriage window
Standing alone at an unfamiliar station,
Who did not turn his head or hear me calling
As the wheels moved on.

He clung to me, his small wet mouth, his heartbeat
Were close to me
But he was not mine.
A wilderness of flying leaves and birds
Lay in between.

(c. 1944).

Poem

My arms are rivers heavy with raw flood,
And their white reaches cry though flesh be dumb,
And I am ill with sudden tenderness
For him – I had not known that such duress
Of thorny sweetness fell to fatherhood.
Arms can be torrents; little creature, come
And in the river-banks of my caress

Find you a coign for conies, or a nest
Under the overhanging of my head
For wildfowl, or curl here, ah close, and be
In hearing of the tides that flood in me,
And listen to the boulders in my breast,
And dare the compass of my arms, nor dread
The pools of shade they spill for you, so gently.

How vernal, how irradiant is his face
Lit up as though by stars or a quick breeze
Of lucent light that nowhere else abides
Save in his features, lambent like a bride's,
And more unearthly than my crass embrace
Can share or hope for now… the rivers freeze…
And my idiot arms fall, heavy, to my sides.

(c. 1944)

The Three

The Three:
The First
Withered with thirst;
His eyes
Are lakes; he lies
In burning sand –
There is no-one to hold his dusty hand.

The Three:
A nectar
In a cut goblet's glitter
Stands by the Second:
There is no sound.
His eyes
Scour his gold domain for Paradise.

The Three:
The Third
In softest cell
Leaps, froglike, at each yell –
His eyes
Glitter with spears
And dance like fireflies.

(c. 1944)

17 years

The Consumptive. Belsen 1945

I

If seeing her an hour before her last
Weak cough into all blackness I could yet
Be held by chalk-white walls, and by the great
Ash coloured bed,
And the pillows hardly creased
By the tapping of her little cough-jerked head –
If such can be a painter's ecstasy,
(Her limbs like pipes, her head a china skull)
Then where is mercy?
And what
Is this my traffic? for my schooled eyes see
The ghost of a great painting, line and hue,
In this doomed girl of tallow?

O Jesus! has the world so white a yellow
As lifts her head by but a breath from linen
In the congested and yet empty world
Of plaster, cotton, and a little marl?
Than pallor what is there more terrible?
There lay the gall
Of that dead mouth of the world.
And at death's centre a torn garden trembled
In which her eyes like great hearts of black water
Shone in their wells of bone,
Brimmed to the well-heads of the coughing girl,
Pleading through history in that white garden;
And very wild, upon the head's cheekbones,
As on high ridges in an icy dew,
Burned the sharp roses.

II

Her agony slides through me: am I glass
That grief can find no grip
Save for a moment when the quivering lip
And the coughing weaker than the broken wing
That, fluttering, shakes the life from a small bird
Caught me as in a nightmare? Nightmares pass;
The image blurs and the quick razor-edge
Of anger dulls, and pity dulls. O God,
That grief so glibly slides! The little badge
On either cheek was gathered from her blood:
Those coughs were her last words. They had no weight
Save that through them was made articulate
Earth's desolation on the alien bed.
Though I be glass, it shall not be betrayed,
That last weak cough of her small, trembling head.

(c. May 1945)

134

This German Pinewood

This German pinewood swam
In a grey dream
Of captured men.
The forest floor was like a waste
Of endless weeds – the prisoners of war
Filled the wide forest's floor
Crushing the forest bed
With leg and flank and hip and breast and head.

(c. May 1945)

The World Is Broken without Love

The world is broken without love
It is forsaken without love.
It is a man without his love,
A girl without her love.

What is the core of Hope save love?
There is no other Faith but love.
O love! there is no other one.
O love, than you, there is no-one
The cold globe aches for love.

What is there left, but love?

(October 1945)

Yet Who to Love Returning

Love is not simple, is not always
Gentle, nor always truthful – O
If love be not so
What is there left to trust these disparate days?

Yet who, to love returning, has not found
Her hushed and green,
And the soul's quarantine
In her deep woods and river-threaded ground.

(October 1945)

Victims

They had no quiet and smoothed sheets of death
To fold them and no pillows whiter than the wings
Of childhood's angels.
There was no hush of love. No silence flowered
About them, and no bland, enormous petals
Opened with stillness. Where was lavender
Or gentle light? Where were the coverlets
Of quiet? Or white hands to hold their bleeding
Claws that grabbed horribly for child or lover?
In twisting flames their twisting bodies blackened,
For History, that witless chronicler
Continued writing his long manuscript.

(c. 1945)

137

Poem

Remote, that baleful head of his,
Suggesting the inordinate moon
It moves upon his neck and has
A cold existence of its own

It is a mountainous and vast
Domain of leather, rock and bone,
And hair, like grass blows from the scalp
Where play the fingers of the sun.

(c. 1945)

All Eden Was Then Girdled by My Arms

All Eden was then girdled by my arms.
The snake, the lady, and the sharp white fruit,
The rhododendron sky and the foam-like plumes
Of dappled fowl that down green zephyrs float.

O wild, wise garden, palpable you lay,
A metamorphosis at my breastbone burning.
The lioness and the white lamb at play
For the last time across the diamond morning.

Within so small a noose my girdling arms
Held you, my sweet, and yet the noose was doom –
Doom in the brain, doom in the ringing limbs
When branches broke and a gold bird flew home.

(c. 1946)

The Vastest Things Are Those We May Not Learn

The vastest things are those we may not learn.
We are not taught to die, nor to be born,
Nor how to burn
With love.
How pitiful is our enforced return
To those small things we are the masters of.

(c. 1946)

Poem

It is at times of half-light that I find
Forsaken monsters shouldering through my mind.
If the earth were lamplit I should always be
Found in their company.

Even in sunlight I have heard them clamouring
About the gateways of my brain, with glimmering
Rags about their bruise-dark bodies bound,
And in each brow a ruby like a wound.

(c. 1946)

140

Each Day We Live Is a Glass Room

I

Each day we live is a glass room
Until we break it with the thrusting
Of the spirit and pass through
The splintered walls to the green pastures
Where the birds and buds are breaking
Into fabulous song and hue
By the still waters.

II

Each day is a glass room unless
We break it: but how rare's the day
We have the power to raise the dead
And walk on air to the green pastures!
For the clouded glass, or clay,
Is blind with usage, though the Lord
Walk the still waters.

(c. 1946)

As a Great Town Draws the Eccentrics In

As a great town draws the eccentrics in,
So am I like a city built of clay
Where madmen flourish, for beneath my skin,
In every secret arch or alleyway

That winds about my bones of midnight, they
Lurk in their rags, impatient for the call
To muster at my breastbone, and to cry
For revolution through the capital.

(c. 1946)

141

Conscious that Greatness Has Its Tinder Here

Conscious that greatness has its tinder here
But that the fire in me through lack of power
To find its golden grip, can never flower
Into the high flame of an oracle –
I drift from day to day, from hour to hour
Yet have not lost the hope of miracle.

And have not lost the hope of miracle
Nor that small moments can be crushed by so
Enormous a contempt (the while they blow
In swarms like insects), by my huge desire
To burn away my spirit in life's bonfire –
And to unlock the secret manacle.

(c. 1946)

The Restaurant

There is more silence here than where the cold
Grey dunes of midnight swell into the stars.
There is more silence here than where a gold
And sterile desert reaches without pause

To the unbroken circle of the sky.
Here among gaudy lights and voices crude,
And the cheap glass clangour of society,
Sudden, has come on me, a solitude

Drenching this tinsel hour in time's great tide –
A garish fragment lost in mountainous seas –
And I am drowned in silence, as I ride
Into the drifting core of dynasties.

(c. 1946)

If Trees Gushed Blood

If trees gushed blood
When they were felled
By meddling man,
And crimson welled

From every gash
His axe can give,
Would he forbear
And let them live?

(c. 1946)

When the Heart Cries in Love

When the heart cries in love all else is over,
The earth is finished and over, all is gone
One cares not where; only the heart beats on,
Bruising the tired breasts of loved and lover.

While the heart cries in love, fields, towns and weather,
Waters and cities falter through the dark
While we, both wide asleep, and fast awake
In eldritch air, cry out for one another.

(c. 1946)

What Is that Noise in the Shaking Trees?

What is that noise in the shaking trees behind
My shoulder blades? it is cold, it is close, it is loud –
What is that sound?

It is the noise of the sea in the leaves of the trees that you hear.

And what is that sound in the crowding waves before
My eyes, a field away, yet loud –
What is that sound?

It is the sound of the leaves in the foliaged sea that you hear.

For the sound of the sea is the noise of the woods tonight
And the noise of the leaves is the sound of the crowding waves
And it is a night when nature arises and grieves
Not knowing herself for what she is or why.

It is water among huge branches tossing
It is a dangerous tide in the branches massing
It is the noise of the waves through foliage passing.

(c. 1946)

Neither to Captain nor be Captained, I

Neither to captain nor be captained, I
Am like the hollow coracle at sea
Across the soul's wide waters drifting witless,
Flying a shadow-flag across the sun.
My inter-changing cargo huge yet weightless –
My lading the brimmed sunlight, or the gloom
Of brackish ballast – oh what vessel's ribs
Knows cargo that can shift its weight like mine,
From radiance to black brine?

(c. 1946)

Crumbles the Crested Scroll

Crumbles the crested scroll across whose onetime
Brilliant breast a monarch scrawled the black
Insect that spoke Empire
The spider of his name.

(c. 1946)

Wayward O World and Unpredictable

Wayward O world and unpredictable –
I glimpse your lusty handling in the theme
Of the great cadence makers. For the youth
Squat as a frog, his mottled jaw awry –
His feet aslither like huge fish can wrench
The pulsing phrase from the dead and dying words
That England spawns in shoals of sound uncharted –
The while the scholar of felicitous tongue,
The classics scheduled in his perfect skull
Dies between lily sheets forgotten – O
Wayward World, Glorious and Impudent
That knows what marl best feeds your Burning Plant.

(c. 1946)

O Love, the World's Solution

O love, the world's solution and the fever
That burns no brow – the burning badge no wearer
Dares to wear always.

(c. 1946)

When Tiger-Men Sat Their Mercurial Coursers

When tiger-men sat their mercurial coursers,
Hauled into shuddering arches the proud fibre
Of head and throat, sank spurs, and trod on air –
    I was not there...

When clamorous centaurs thundered to the rain-pools,
Shattered with their fierce hooves the silent mirrors,
When glittering drops clung to their beards and hair –
    I was not there...

When through a blood-dark dawn a man with antlers
Cried, and throughout the day the echoes suffered
His agony and died in evening air –
    I was not there.

(c. 1946)

This Field Is Dim with Sheaves

This field is dim with sheaves – the next
Is furrowed with dark lines; beside
It spreads a narrow stippled field
That meets a meadow bare and wide –
Ah Lord!
How faultlessly the fields are spread abroad!

This season trembles with green birth –
Beyond it the thick summer stands
Against a season of strange breath
That meets a season of stretched hands –
Ah Lord!
How startling are the seasons spread abroad!

(c. 1946)

Brave Lies Conspiring in the Three-Hued Flag

Brave lies conspiring in the three-hued flag
Drag at my vision; for the cornflower eyes
And tousled locks of boys confuse the rag
Of rhetoric with Galahad chivalries.

Lies interweave and burrow through my world
Of erstwhile adamantine faith; they pock
The crystal and the yellowest inch of gold
And smear their evil on my peerless rock.

Pluck lies out of your entrails as they grow.
Make yourself light, light and with only truth
(Heavy enough as ballast) steadying you
And move into a world of fearless growth.

Run through the three-hued flag and for your part
Take no crude stain. Run whitely through loud camps
And in the shuffling landscape of your heart
Hold close to you your dazzling ace of trumps.

(c. 1946)

Are We Not the Richer?

Are we not the richer
Who have suffered the shadow?
Who have stood sky-staring in the naked field,
No, not for benediction,
But more proudly,
Awaiting, as at bay
The approaching cloud
Of alien metal.

Are we not the richer
Who have seen our loves
Loading the fickle scales
Who have stared unseeing
At a shifting fulcrum?

We who have fed
On anguish; who have wondered
Whether to plant a flower,
Whether to smile,
Were mockery,
O island people!
Surely we are the richer
Who have tasted tension!

(c. 1946)

The Pit-Boy's Lung Is Black

The pit-boy's lung is black with what
He wins the sunk day through.
And while you warm your delicate hands
His lung is black for you.

He rises to the windy light,
The negro of cold Wales –
And in his dark throat leaps the lyric
Fire of her nightingales.

(c. 1946)

Crisis

In crimson tatters this my orphan heart
Treads, treads the metal highway of my days,
Spreads, spreads her blood red wings above the heel
But cannot lift me.

Here, while the dagger hangs, O Absalom!
The images crowd in and blind the eyes,
The tatters flaunt their fire; a heritage
Of pain cries, 'Wonder!'

This is the day of days! The empires hang.
Columbus finds us shrivelled to a marble.
We choose betwixt the mole and the strong eyes
Of the stark falcon. Crammed with destinies;
Ours is the fulcrum.

Not ours the hands for the dark reins. Not ours
The throats to cry 'Unleash' or 'Leash', we stand
Magnificent, the sky's black cloud impending,
And at our feet, imperilled, and O, tender,
Gather our loves.

(c. 1946)

151

It Is the Malady

It is the Malady.
What ship upon what sea
Tosses, as tosses now
My heart where no winds blow?

How strangely shot with light
Such waters are, where night
And day across the brine
Disclaim the sun and moon.

(c. 1946)

At My Inmost Heart Is Fear

At my inmost heart is fear
For the death of all that's dear
Must surely come:
Every joy and every bliss
Close their petals at my kiss.
At my inmost heart is this
Prescience of the tomb.

Would I were all radiance through;
Would I were a glittering hue;
A spangled man!
Would I were an empty clown,
Eyed with stars in a gold town!
Even so, my heart would drown
In laughter not its own.

(c. 1946)

153

This Is the Darkness

This is the darkness: I have known great storms
Scourge the long day – but this is motionless
And sterile: this is something featureless
The blind brain turning upon drugs and worms.

(c. 1946)

I Cannot Find It in Me to Be Gay

I cannot find it in me to be gay.
I think I am the godchild of those clouds
Which weep and weep and never lift away –
Or of such marshland trees
As cannot dry their eyes.

I think I am the foster-child of Sorrow
For only on dark evenings when the sky
Gives heavy presage of a rainy morrow
Am I at one with all
That's rare and magical.

(c. 1946)

There Is No Difference between Night and Day

There is no difference between night and day
For time is darkness now, halted and null.
The roads of noon lead their abstracted way,
The beasts of midnight wander through the skull.

Darkness and time have fused and formed a circle
Around the little gestures of the clay
And there's no movement but the papery cycle
Of calendars whose cold leaves float away.

(c. 1946)

The Heart Holds Memories Older than the Mind's

When beauty rides into the hollow heart
It is as something that comes home again
As though for anchorage; or like a reckless
Prodigal returning to his father
Up dappled aisles of immemorial cedars.

When a great beauty silences the heart
And holds it spellbound, it is recognition
Of something half remembered, long before
Atlantis was, when love was the wild fruit
We fed upon in golden climes forgotten.

(c. 1946)

Lug Out Your Spirit from Its Cage of Clay

Lug out your spirit from its cage of clay!
Let it have air before its feathers fade.
When will your body and your brain obey
The burning fowl and scorn to be afraid?

And scorn to be afraid, for it will lead
You from the body's darkness into the day –
And smash the mouldering bars of thought and deed,
Lug out your spirit from its cage of clay!

(c. 1946)

There Is an Aristocracy of Love

There is an aristocracy of love
Rarer than chemicals – slow in its golden
Measures; like deep waters; heard with sight
And seen with hearing.

(c. 1946)

Poem

How dangerous a thing to fill man's inches of earth with life!
So huge a thing to charge the clay with, Lord.
Surely You played with fire, with more than fire,
With something fiercer, something that leaped higher
And threw its long and flickering shadow further
Than Your own wisdom knew. How dangerous,
Incalculable, feckless and explosive
For such a little vessel!

(c. 1946)

Into the Sky All Men Must Turn Their Eyes

Into the sky all men must turn their eyes.
Let it be full of pain; of dying things
The mouths of those who mourn – the hands of babies
Bleeding among the stars
Load up the sky's white canvas face with them
And carve them from the dark clouds to our shame,
The shapes of the torn heart

(c. 1946)

And I Thought You beside Me

And I thought you beside me
How rare and how desperate
And your eyes were wet
And your face as still
As the body of a leveret
On a tranced hill
But my thought belied me
And you were not there
But only the trees that shook,
Only a storm that broke
Through the dark air.

(c. 1946)

Into the Dusky Well

Into the dusky well
Of English words
I dip
My wavering pitcher
For those, which, at the lip
Of sound, set in fresh sequence, will
Enrich her
Wild heritage
Upon a little page.

(c. 1946)

Peake.

Satan

Sickened by virtue he rebelled and cried
For all things horrible to be his bride

For through the hot red tides of sin move such
Fish as lose radiance at virtue's touch.

Should he reform and vomit up his evil?
It would not only be that his spiked devil

Would be dethroned, but also, amid groans
Those swarming hues that make his joints their homes.

(c. 1946)

Features Forgo Their Power

Features forgo their power
To quicken or darken:
Cold and exact they lie
Where there is none to waken.

Only the fluttering dies.
The motionless mouth,
The brow, and the upturned eyes
Have their separate death.

The living tear and the lashes
Black and wet
Immemorial are
In the grief they stir.

The love and the anger live
But are far away:
Life was so nervously wove
Through her delicate clay.

159

More rare… more rare
Than thought can well hold
Were the dawns and the dusks of that zephyr'd head
That lolls in the cold.

Most far… most far,
From the white host now –
Its guesthood ended, the flower
Floats from the bough.

(c. 1946)

Let Dreams Be Absolute

Let dreams be absolute. The yellow horse
Is not a thing of mist – it drops its armoured
Hooves through shallows that are blind with sand,
Its fetlocks floating like white seaweeds rooted
To the great ankle that conveys them down
To where the whorled shells sleep.

Let dreams be absolute; I crave a life
Of imaginative growth from day to day,
Heart, brain, and mind so that when I have failed –
As fail all those who clutch the smarting stars –
I will at least when dying
Remember how my dreams were absolute.

(c. 1946)

The Birch Saplings

So vulnerably young and sickle naked,
As slight as breastless girls, their slightness gleaming
In pallid atmosphere, the saplings send
Their jets of nakedness like notions upwards.

O! they will find the world is full of rancour
And treachery and that their slenderness
Will wake no pity in the surging seasons
Of drought and frost and flood and clinging ice –
No love in the totalitarian weather.

(c. 1946)

His Head and Hands Were Built for Sin

I

His head and hands were built for sin,
As though predestined from the womb
They had no choice: an earthish doom
Has dogged him from his fortieth gloom
Back to where glooms begin.

II

That skull, those eyes, that lip-less mouth,
That frozen jaw, that ruthless palm
Leave him no option but to harm
His fellows and be harmed by them.
The beast his marrow feeds must wander forth.

III

If he die this way or die that,
If he be hung or end between
Torn blankets in a rented den,
Yet his last heart-beat will have been
The knell of something separate,

IV

Fled, like the unicorn, away,
For ever gone, that was alone,
Loveless, unique as fire or stone,
Lone victim of primordial bone,
Earth's quarry with the earth for prey.

V

Hell's dice were thrown. It was not he
Who carved his brow's crude beetling size
Or scooped the caverns for his eyes
Where squat the hatreds: let the wise
Recall the fanged caves of the sea.

VI

His thudding heart is drawn and driven
By rhythms as immemorial as
The tides of the moon: and dangerous,
And naked as their waves he is,
And as innocent in the shrewd eye of heaven.

(c. 1946)

I Have Become Less Clay than Hazel-Rod

I have become less clay than hazel-rod,
For to the great lake of your graciousness
The tremors bend:
And the diviner's fist, my double-yard
Of earth's become, to clutch the alchemies
And make an end.

Unless the warlock loose the straining
Rod, the emerald hazel cracks
Death at the palm.
Unless your shrouded waters bring
Love's climbing wave, wherefore this stick
Of splintered doom?

(c. 1946)

Cold Island! The Splenetic Air

1

Cold Island! the splenetic air
Is icicled with light and bells
Clang through the blood; the hair
Screams from the scalp; the grey
Shoal of an aqueous mist among the hazels
Has come to stay.

2

Cold Island; in the gold, unbroken South
The mountains stutter when a jaguar yells
For Africa has fire in her mouth.
But we are closer to the arctic bone,
As standing here among the shaking hazels
Our north is known.

(c. 1946)

Rembrandt

The tawny darkness, goldness, the black earth;
Brocades of loaded pigment; the pale light
That drags a swallow'd forehead from the night,
And urges wrinkled fingers into birth
From a dark womb of canvas; and the graved
Decipherable words that ring old eyes:
The lure of all flesh smoulders from the thighs,
The breasts and from the arms Suzanna laved.

Gizzard or silk, bread for the miller's youth;
A hotter grist for his tremendous milling.
Matter itself: the clamorous ghetto; filling
His heart with swords and turbans of thick truth

Until death laid him in a pauper's grave,
Gulfed in those shadows that his pictures have.

(c. 1946)

Victoria Station. 6.58 p.m.

Sudden, beneath the pendant clock arose
Out of the drab and artificial ground
A horse with wings of scarlet, and pale flowers
Glimmered upon his forehead, while around

His neck and mane like wreaths of incense streamed
Young hosts of stars, and as his eyes burned proud,
The men with black umbrellas stood and stared
And nudged each other, and then laughed aloud.

(c. 1946)

165

Half-Light

Why do you leave me now when such strange beauty
Defies me, at the turning of your head,
So dim; in half-light on the moth-dark bed,
You lie and watch me watch you. Alien
You are become when you have carved a glory
Out of your flesh and blood.
And when
You move such carving on the pillows ghostly
And do not know it, then
Our love is worthless, broken apart, and dead
For lack of unimaginable magic –
Ah, you smile –
Unwittingly you smile
And draw me in,
(Tearing tremendous wings from off my back)
Out of a region that was fierce and lonely.

(c. 1946)

How Shall I Find Me

I

How shall I find me, so that I may bend
My powers to one end
And be
Conscious of wading in the waves of me?

II

How shall I find me, so that I may run
Over these sands of dawn, until comes on
Twilight from noon,
And see my climax in the golden moon?

(c. 1946)

Let the Result Be What It May

Let the result be what it may, I have launched my ship
To keel what seas I know not, nor may guess
How deep will be that final wilderness
Where she shall let her last black anchor slip.

Under the fitful stars that gleam and drip
Down the dank wall of an enormous sky.
Or where the sun stabs like an enemy
With burning splinters and I long to die –
Or where the cold ghosts cry…

Let the result be what it may, I have launched my ship.

(c. 1946)

Sark; Evening

1

From the sunset I turn away
To the sweep of a steel bay.

2

The lonely waters are grander far
Than the red and gold are.

(c. 1946)

That Phoenix Hour

When I take
Strong bread and break
Its body white,
Then strange and bright
My hands become,
And I have power
And suffer doom
That phoenix hour.

(c. 1946)

Robert Frost

The great tree creaked and splinters of sharp ice
Broke from the frozen branches in a shower;
I thought of Robert Frost and of his power
With simple words that he can so entice
And wake
To such a startling order; they can bring
Fresh grass up wet against the heart and slake
My English dust with his New England spring.

(c. 1946)

The Wings

There is no way into the silver cloud
Save by long battle with the wings that cry –
That wither up and rot, unless the proud
Spirit fight on, until they scorn the sky.

For only when the wings beat thinnest air
Can the eye see the pattern of the mind;
Only when stars are burning in the hair,
The heart may ponder and the heart may find.

(c. 1946)

Written About a Piece of Paper when About to Draw

This is my world! to make or mar, my world!
Here with my slender weapon I announce
My pulse-beat in the lead – and here unfurled
Toss my grey flags.

(c. 1946)

169

As Battle Closes In My Body Stoops

As battle closes in my body stoops
Exulting from the zenith as I fall
To the steel ceiling of their turret tops.
Spread-eagled over tanks like toys I sprawl
On the hot fumes of war, and as men die
I gather them into my smile of gall.

Lolling on senseless massacre I lie
Capacious while the innumerable dead
From battlefields and cities rise to me.
Death, the unrivalled of our century;
Death, for whose midnight kiss your child was bred.

(c. 1946)

When All Is Said and Done

When all is said and done
And the philosophic argument lost and won
England at war has found, once more, her brave
And quizzical son
And sent him to his grave

(c. 1946)

Possessionless, O Leveret

Possessionless, O leveret!
Scorner of warrens, like a ghost
You lie upon the sloping cold
Of the great hillside.
At your first movement in the dew
Of dawn the vase of reason cracks
From side to side.

You are the fable of dim feet,
You are the grey ghost, leveret,
Come dog, come rider, you are fleet,
And if they kill you, leveret

Your upland ghost evades them yet,
Your wasteland spirit, leveret.

(c. 1946)

Love So Imperilled Is

Love so imperilled is
By words within its boundaries
Stalking:
However rare the cadences,
There's death in talking.

I have known love halt and shiver
At the touch of words that never
So deftly wove
Their message like a summer river –
Quiver and die, because no language
Suffers love.

(c. 1946)

Love's House

What if the stones
Of our Love are strong?
What if the foundations
Are on granite?

It is no solace
When the windows are broken
And the floorboards glitter
With jagged glass.

What if the roof
Withstands the gales,
If the tears of the rain
Seep endlessly?

What use is the strength
Of our stone built house?
If the rain runs over
Its motionless face?

What if the stones
Of our house are strong?
Strength, in itself
Has no strength at all.

(c. 1946)

The Flag Half-Masted Is a People's Poem

The flag half-masted is a people's poem –
How naked is the uppermast in air!
How empty the high mast-head pitiful!
Though who has died the crowd is unaware.

Is it the symbol that holds tragedy?
The toys of the dead child float sea-grief under,
O heart! half-masted heart! run up your ensign.
No, not in truth but in its ghost is wonder.

(c. 1946)

Love, I Had Thought It Rocklike

I

Love, I had thought it rocklike,
Rooted, and foursquare,
But it was a bird of the air,
Restless, winged for flying,
Delicate and perilously rare.

II

The last of a species;
Or a last duet
Of lovers, of birds –
The last of all lyrics,
Its blue ink drying
On a poet's words.

III

I had thought that it stood
But it slithered like sand;
I had thought it founded
Like a city of stone –
But it was thistledown
Or the touch of a wand.

IV

I had thought it solid,
The sun on it burning,
A planted thing –
Love's minster, ageless,
Its rich pipes turning
The stones to gold –
But it was slight,
Airborne and exquisite,
Half tethered, half running –
A heart-shaped kite
On the wings of the world.

V

It was a leaf of the aspen,
It was not the aspen.
A ripple of the ocean,
It was not the ocean.
It was a bird on a rooted rock
And birds are rootless.

VI

And in some other climate of the heart
It stands upon a cold, illusory shore,
Or floats, O feckless,
Now and for ever
Over weird water.

(c. 1946)

Swans Die and a Tower Falls

Swans die and a tower falls.
Light crumbles in lost halls
Where effigies
Stare from marmoreal eyes
Until the masonry
About them drops away
And they are ruined
Among wilds of wind,
And light breaks in again
In vain… in vain,
For love has fled and where it was
Mouths pain.

Swans die, and a tower falls,
And our cities hear cold bells
Toll the nepenthe
Of earth, air, and sea,
Flesh, fish and bird,
Morality and amorality,
Ploughshare and sword
World without end…
Then laugh! and laugh again
Before the end
Of our fleet span, sweet friend!
O my sweet friend!

(c. 1946)

And Are You Then Love's Spokesman in the Bone?

And are you then Love's spokesman in the bone?
For there's a raging orator whose yell
Startles the sleeping jaw from ear to chin.
If you *are* he, cease cryer! for too well
I know your voice – and what it is you mean.
And there's no need to tell me what I own,

For it is love I own, and you must go.
Your voice along the victim jaw-bone stuttering
Has stabbed its message dry. What need is there
To add so crude a pain to all the fluttering
Madness of the heart – O orator!
Silence your voice: you serve no purpose now.

(c. 1946)

For Ever through Love's Weather Wandering

1

All bearings lost in this so great a fever:
For ever through love's weather wandering,
Un-piloted – yet send me back, no never
To where the north star shines. No compass bring

2

Me now: Smash all their needles – this is magic.
(Can you not hear love's vast, archaic music?)
All bearings gone: only the frigate heart
Lost in a leaping ocean of red light.

(c. 1946)

The Rhyme of the Flying Bomb

A babe was born in the reign of George
To a singular birth-bed song,
Its boisterous tune was off the beat
And all of its words were wrong;

But a singular song it was, for the house
As it rattled its ribs and danced,
Had a chorus of doors that slammed their jaws
And a chorus of chairs that pranced.

And the thud of the double-bass was shot
With the wail of the floating strings,
And the murderous notes of the ice-bright glass
Set sail with a clink of wings –

Set sail from the bursted window-frame
To stick in the wall like spears,
Or to slice off the heads of the birthday flowers
Or to nest on a chest-of-drawers.

And a hurdling siren wailed with love
And the windows bulged with red,
And the babe that was born in the reign of George
Wailed back from its raddled bed.

And its mother died when the roof ran in
And over the counterpane,
And the babe that was born in the reign of George
Was found in a golden drain,

Was found in a fire-bright drain asleep
By a sailor dazed and lost
In a waterless world where the searchlights climbed
The sky with their fingers crossed.

Through streets where the little red monkey-flames
Run over the roofs and hop
From beam to beam, and hang by their tails
Or pounce on a table-top –

Through streets where the monkey-flames run wild
And slide down the banisters,
The sailor strode with the new-born babe
To the hiss of the falling stars.

Through streets where over the window-sills
The loose wallpapers pour
And ripple their waters of nursery whales
By the light of a world at war;

And ripple their wastes of bulls and bears
And their meadows of corn and hay
In a harvest of love that was cut off short
By the scythe of an ape at play –

Through the scarlet streets and the yellow lanes
And the houses like shells of gold
With never a sign of a living soul
The sailor carried the child.

And a ton came down on a coloured road,
And a ton came down on a gaol,
And a ton came down on a freckled girl,
And a ton on the black canal,

And a ton came down on a hospital,
And a ton on a manuscript,
And a ton shot up through the dome of a church,
And a ton roared down to the crypt.

And a ton danced over the Thames and filled
A thousand panes with stars,
And the splinters leapt on the Surrey shore
To the tune of a thousand scars.

And the babe that was born in the reign of George
Lay asleep in the sailor's arm,
With the bombs for its birthday lullaby
And the flames for its birthday dream.

The sailor looked down at the doll in the crook
Of his arm with a salty sigh,
It was naked and red as a rose in the light
Of a last low evening ray.

And he lifted the wrinkled doll in his hand
Like a watch to his frost-bit ear,
And he heard the tick of its heart beat quick
On the drum as he held it there.

'What kind of a lark is this?' he said,
'And what'll I do? To hell
With finding a babe in a golden drain
With its ticker at work 'n all.

'I would rather my god-damn sea of salt
That is master of bomb an' fire,
Though it stung my heart when it drowned my mate
In the thick of its midnight hair.

'I would rather the sea that can sting the heart
In a way I can understand
Than this London raw as an open sore
And a new-born babe in my hand.'

The sailor strode over the glittering glass
A-dazzle with jags of red
And came to a man leaning over a wall
With his shadow above his head.

'Can you tell me the nearest First Aid Post?'
The sailor said to the man,
But the lounging figure made no reply
For the back of his head was gone.

The sailor wiped the sweat from his face
And he laughed in a hapless way.
'O Christ! little fish,' he said to the babe,
'This isn't no place to stay.

'This isn't no place for the likes of you
Nor it is for the likes of me.
We'd be better asleep in a hammock, we would,
On the wet of the mine-filled sea.

'We'd be far better off where the soldiers are
Than naked in London town
Where a house can rock like a rocking-horse
And the bright bricks tumble down.

'All bare and cold in that gutter of gold
You had no cause to be,
No more than it's right for the likes of you
To be born in this century.

'But the sky is bright though it's late at night
And the colours are gay as gay
And the glass that is lodged in my hip bone now
Is jabbing from far away.

'And the warding off of that burning beam
Has hurt my shoulder sore,
And I want to laugh! O my little blind fish!
And dance on the golden floor.

'See! See! Ha! Ha! how the dazzling streets
Are empty from end to end
With only a cat with a splinter through its heart,
And an arm where the railings end.'

And the sailor threw back his head and laughed
In a way that was loud and torn,
And even his mother would never have guessed
That his face was the face of her son.

And over his mind like a flutter of leaves
His scare-crow memories fell
And the light in his eye was the wrecker's light
That burns on the wharves of hell.

And his dance was a scare-crow dance, and his feet
Clashed loud on the streets of glass,
And his bones shone red and were sticky with his blood
While he signed for the ships to pass.

And the ships of brick and the ships of stone
And the charcoal ships lurched by
While his footsteps clashed on the frozen waves
That shone to the scarlet sky.

While raised aloft and for'ard of his heart
Like a small, bright figurehead,
Lay the babe in the crib of his bowsprit arm,
Asleep like a babe in bed.

Like a babe in the cot of a golden storm
It opened its new-born eye
To the shuffle of the warm, red, restless air
And the dazzle of the witchcraft sky.

'Watch me! watch me!' cried the man from the sea
With his long and scare-crow legs,
As he leapt like a spider on the foreign shore
Of a million coral-jags.

And he pranced like a spider through the fire-torn door
Of a church where a headless horse
Lay stiff in the smouldering aisle with a hoof
At its heart like the sign of the cross.

And he leapt the horse with a mantis leap,
And he came to the front row pew
And he laid the babe on the charcoal bench
And he turned to where the pulpit grew.

It grew from a mound of tapers and stones
And bibles and deep blue glass,
But its carven top had been left by the bomb
Exactly as it always was.

But the steps were gone and he swarmed the side
Like a pilot and came aboard
And stood for a moment with his heavy hands
On the gull-winged word of God.

And there, below, like a spark of light
In the deep of the church was the babe
With its new-born eyes wide open on his own
And its hands on the charcoal slab.

And lo, from the bedlam sky had flown
The last black bomber away
And the air was quiet in the crag-walled church
And the dawn was an hour away.

'O my little bright fish!' the sailor cried
In a voice as gruff as a gun,
'Shall I worship you now from this crow's-nest here
In the silence what's just begun?

'Shall I worship you now for your brand-new look
And your brand-new arms and legs
And your fists like a brace of anemones,
And your body as soft as an egg?

'O, Christ in heaven! I must worship you
For the ticker you keep in your chest;
I must worship you for your new-look, babe,
That'll never be washed or dressed.

'With the light of your eyes so fixed on mine
Then strong as a lion I am!
The lion of Judah, or Africa,
Or the one that lay down with the lamb.

'O watch me quick! for my mane burns thick
With its locks of yellow and black!
The world that lopes through the night above
Can never come loping back.'

The sailor jumped with a single jump
And stood on the pulpit's rim,
'Now listen to me while I sing you a tale
To the tune of a bleeding hymn!

'For the things I've forgotten for many a year
Are shouldering into my mind,
Of the time when my heart was a wave that heaved
To the gale of my sea-mad mind.'

He spread out his hands like a starfish brown
At the sides of his big rough head;
'Will you listen to me, my finless fish
As you lie on your wrinkled bed?'

'I will! I will!' came a cry as shrill
And thin as river-reed,
'I am wide awake and the church is still,
O sailor I will indeed.

'I will! I will!' cried the new-born babe,
'Though I've lived it all before,
For there's nothing new when the womb is through
With its restless prisoner.'

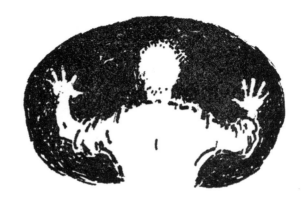

And the babe sprang up on the charcoal pew
And stretched out its wrinkled arms,
O, a sprite it was, or a gull or a frog
Or a grape or a bud as it blooms.

'O listen my sailor, saviour man,
Though the world is a place that's wide,
There's nothing outside of the womb of Eve
That you wouldn't have known inside.

'If you tell me a tale I shall listen well
To the roll of your salt-sea voice –
But I'd rather be singing along with you
As we sang in the early days.

'For, sailor, there's nothing that is not true
If it's true to your heart and mine
From a unicorn to a flying bomb
From a wound to a glass of wine.'

'O my new-born sprite with your eyes alight
Be careful as you call!
I wouldn't have you crash upon the cold, stone floor
With your limbs so soft and small.'

The new-born babe soared up in the air
To the head of a candlestick
Where it hovered with its hands clenched tight at its breast
At the height of the gull-winged Book.

'I have swarmed the masts of a thousand fleets,
I have drowned through the bruise-blue sea,
I have burned through an age of scarlet fires
So have no fear of me.'

'Ahoy then! my cockleshell babe aloft
On your candlestick mast so high!
What a time we'd have had all over the world
On the waters of yesterday!'

'I remember well!' cried the hovering babe,
'I remember everything;
You have only to sing, my war-time friend,
And I will know what to sing.'

Then the sailor lifted his deep-sea voice,
And the naked babe cried shrill
Of a day that had been in the sailor's blood
For as long as his heart could tell –

Of a day that was far away in his blood
But as close as breath to the babe
And as vivid to each as the fires that night
Or the blood of the London curb.

And the song flew on like a hundred songs
That grow in the brain like grass:
'It was long ago, it was long ago
Or ever the world war was.'

'It was long ago,' cried the voice of the babe,
'Far further than yesterday.'
And the sailor cried, 'It was long ago
And a million miles away.'

And as they sang a cold light ran
From the east of London town
And shone upon the horse with its hoof at its heart
And the hymn books crisp and brown.

'O sailor, saviour, the dawn is up!
And the fires are dying down;
What a lovely light for my birthday bright
With the birds of iron flown.'

But the scare-crow sailor made no reply,
For his limbs shook suddenly
And the golden fume that had filled his brain
Slid cruelly away.

Then the babe, with a leap was at his side
And had knelt on the Holy Word –
'I am frightened, little fish, O what can it be
That my heart beats high and hard!

'And my strength is ebbing away from me
And the lion in my breast has died,
O what can it be that from head to foot
I am now so terrified?'

'Step down from the pulpit's walnut rim,'
Said the voice of the infant child,
'And join your hands by the side of the word
While the light of the dawn is spilled;

'For your brain is alone now your passion goes,
And your coloured dreams run cold
And there's nothing left but a gaping skull
On the spine of the wounded world.

'But we are well! O sailor! sailor!
O we are very well!
Do not tremble as you stand, O frightened sailor
For death is so mean and small.

'It snatches away the burning breath
And it snatches at the useless clay
But what can it do to halt the square-rigged
Soul as it steers away?'

'What use is my soul,' cried the trembling sailor,
'When my breath is torn away?
O naked babe who can speak like a man
Have you nothing but that to say?'

'O sailor, saviour, you rescued me
And I would not have you cry.
If you have no Faith yet your act was Love,
The greatest of the three.

'And out of your love, O frightened sailor
You showed me the coloured lights,
And the golden shoals of the falling stones,
And the scarlet of the streets;

'And I am rich on my natal day
With such rare tragedy
That I have no fear, but only long
That you could be rich like me.

'And I who have died a thousand times
Will cheer you as you die –
O hark! how the sirens wail to us
From Dover by the sea.

'Let us lure them here, the returning raiders –
Oh let us lure them here!
That we may explode in one flash of love
At the height of a world at war.

'For the steed of God has died in the aisle
And the stained glass glowers blue,
I have lived so deep in this natal day
That there is no more to know.'

But the sailor cried, 'O child, if it's true
That you've lived all this before,
What kind of comfort is that to me
Who can never come back for more?

'I am no magical thing like you
And half of my life has gone;
You can speak like a man, and perch in the air,
Though you've only been four hours born,

'But I am not ready to die, O child,
I am not ready to die.
Dear Christ, if my hands and my eyes were gone
I would not be ready to die.'

Down the burning cheek of the naked babe
A tear slid heavily
As though it were taking the curve of the world –
And then, as the stillness lay

Like a throbbing weight, the low sun shone
On the ruins that hemmed them in,
The babe who was born in the reign of George
Knelt down on the pulpit's rim.

'What instrument can measure the Grace
Of God?' the new-born said,
'Or prove the truth of your earthless soul
Until your body is dead?

'There is no proof that the flames to-night
So tall and so luminous
Were as rare as the colours of Zion are
Where the flocks of Jesus graze –

'Nor is there proof that you rescued me
Because of the love of God.
O sailor, sailor, there is no proof
Until your body is dead.'

'But my body is what has laughed for me!
And my body is what has cried!
Where are the tears of my spirit, child?
And how are its cheekbones dried?

'These hands of mine I can understand
Far more than a ransomed soul,
This mouth has crushed the reddest lips
That ever blazed on a girl...'

But as he spoke the wailing broke
Out louder and more loud,
From town to town the banshee cried
Out of the morning cloud.

From town to town the sirens passed
The news of death's approach
Until the warm air leapt like waves
Within the ruined church.

And then, a sudden silence fell
Upon the house of God
And, in the silence... presently...
A ticking sound was heard.

And louder, louder, momently,
Until the ticking was
The stuttering of a far machine
Intent upon its course.

And then, across the thickening air –
'Look! look! O sailor! see!
Who is it stands and wrings her hands
Beside the molten Tree?'

O terrible! Incalculable!
Christ's Mother! The long sound
Of hammers in the London sky
Beats on the open wound.

'Can you not see her? Sailor, saviour,
With the rubble at her feet?
Or hear above the flying Bomb
The huge beats of her heart?'

'My blood has filled my broken shoes
And I am too weak to see
The Virgin now or any ghost
I am so ill and dizzy...

'I am too sick to hear a heart
Beat in a phantom's body –
O tell me, little fish, how long
Before I have to die?'

'Not long, not long, the engine claws
God's face and tears His hands,
O saviour, sailor, take me down
To where his Mother stands.

'She cannot see: her hands are clenched
Across her eyes, the swords
Of Love have driven her so far
Along so many roads.

'Through history, from Bethlehem
Is far to walk alone.
One thousand and nine hundred years
And forty-one, are gone...'

And closer sped the flying cross:
The rattling of its throat
Tossed up the air and shook the shell
Of heaven's battered fort.

The sailor held the new-born sprite,
Fresh mint of George's reign –
And swarming deckwards through the storm
His joy returned again –

His joy returned – his brain broke loose,
And scampered far away.
'Now God be praised,' he yelled, 'the ships
Of hell are in the bay!

'A hundred thousand fire-green crows
Are perched upon the spars
And croak at me, "O sailor see
The brilliance of our claws.

'"We are the long lost tribe of all
That you've been waiting for!"
How glorious it is to sway
Upon the waves of war!

'The masts are bright with silver light,
The decks are black with grass
And the bay's so smooth that I can see
The blood beneath the glass.

'And here's a child, and there's a child
Running across the bay.
They laugh and shout, "Look out! look out!
We haven't long to stay!"

'And here's a man who somersaults
Across the mid-mast air.
The long-shore flames leap out to sea
And drag him by the hair.

'And the guns that shine with oil and wine
Are smothered in sea-flowers deep,
And in the throat of every gun
A mermaid lies asleep.

'And the figurehead with mouth so red
Is drinking up the sea...
O little babe, why won't you leap
Aboard, and sail with me?'

'I will,' the new-born babe replied,
'O sailor, I will, and more –
But hark! the *silence* of the cross
That we've been waiting for.'

A long black wall like a rotting sail
Stood waving to and fro.
It was as though the heavy air
Pressed upwards from below.

It waved and waved and could not fall
Through such portentous air,
While silence like a ghost let down
The long ice of its hair.

When the dead horse rose on its armoured feet
And strode to where they stood,
The crash of its hooves on the hollow stones
Was like the gongs of God.

And the babe slid out of the sailor's coat
And hovered over his head,
And the blood of the babe was mixed with the oozing
Flow of the sailor's blood.

When the silence broke and the air was filled
With the whirr of the diving cross
While the babe hung poised and the fainting sailor
Leaned on the headless horse.

And the church leapt out of a lake of light
And the pews were rows of fire,
And the golden cock crowed thrice and flew
From the peak of the falling spire.

And the candlewax swam over the stones,
And the tail of the flying Bomb
Stuck out of the floor to point the place
That it had journeyed from.

While plunged below in the shattered crypt
Was the skull of the scalding head,
And the short black wings that made the cross
Were splashed with the sailor's blood.

And the dust rose up from the hills of brick
And hung over London town,
And a thousand roofs grew soft and thick
With the dust as it settled down.

And the morning light shone clear and bright
On a city as gold as grain,
While the babe that was born in the reign of George
Lay coiled in the womb again.

(c. 1947)

To the Illegitimate of War

Sired under hedgerows, O
Myriad infants whom
War has engendered.
Sired in the midnight
Alley, O
Children of the world's
Blackout, you
Are the theme of this,
A dedicated list
Of words my flowing heart
Cannot desist.

O welcome! welcome!
Out of the hedgerow lust
The hay-rick love
The hillside play
The blackout opportunity
The endless coincidence of every day
You sprang. Your father, War.
O sudden lust, O tender, tender love
Flowering in times we are not masters of –
O welcome, little children,
Dance, and play.

(c. 1947)

Truths Have no Separate Fires
but from Their Welding

Truths have no separate fires but from their welding
Flames rise, and when the incongruous is found
Not to be so, then, if the gold's no gilding,
Great tombs take wing
From what was burial ground.

The eye, the ear, the intelligence, the spirit,
Through cornucopias of living dream
Veering unburdened, find the heart inherits
The matrix through a drawing in of threads
To the bright destination of a sunbeam
That burns at stairhead,
Flowers in the gloom,
Glowers in the wine
Or, where a field of bread
Sways its pale head,
Creates the sudden signature and sign.

(c. 1948)

Poem

He moves along the bleak, penumbral shire,
His body smouldering with long diamonds
Of silver, yellow, and of sea-green fire,
And at his heels are hunger's restless hounds.

Skyline to skyline – darkness. In his hands
Nothing to hold, and in his eyes no light.
He is the harlequin of broken lands
Wandering forgotten through the martial night.

(c. 1948)

An Ugly Crow Sits Hunched on Jackson's Heart

An ugly crow sits hunched on Jackson's heart
And when it spreads its wings like broken fans
The body of his gloom is torn apart

Revealing sea-green pastures and gold towns
And tents and children climbing to the sun
And all the white and crimson of the clowns.

But Jackson knows no secret way to turn
His tongue into crow-language, nor to plead
His right to pastures, tumblers, and gold towns;

The sullen fowl is witless that it broods
Upon a human heart, and that its wings
When spread disclose his childhood in a flood

Of spectral gold, where fleeting vistas float
Their dappled meads and vales through Jackson's heart.

(1948)

Poem

As much himself is he as Caliban
Is Caliban or Ariel, Ariel.
I shook with jealousy to see a man
Strut with such bombast to his burial.

Loathing my piebald heart that strikes ambiguous
Chords in my breast,
I watched him spit the bright pips as he stalked
Into the darkness like a golden beast.

(1948)

Snow in Sark

The island has become waist-deep in snow –
The ravenous starlings wheel and swarm and flow,
Fighting among the rocks, half tame with hunger,
Half crazed with it. The cries of fear and anger
From birds still strong enough to cry, are thin
Like needles through the falling snow. The whine
Of an icy wind in caves cathedral cold
Echoes along the winter sands, a world
Of spectral beauty. To its edges crawl
Great networks of grey brine, shawl after shawl
Of darkness like a funeral of the tide,
While the gaunt island, glittering like a bride
In dazzling vestment, shines fantastically
Upon her father's arm, the dark-browed sea.

(c. 1948)

Poem

I

The paper is breathless
Under the hand
And the pencil is poised
Like a warlock's wand

II

But the white page darkens
And is blown on the wind
And the voice of a pencil
Who can find?

(c. 1948)

Conceit

I heard a winter tree in song:
Its leaves were birds, a hundred strong;
When all at once it ceased to sing,
For every leaf had taken wing.

(c. 1948)

Out of the Chaos of My Doubt

Out of the chaos of my doubt
And the chaos of my art
I turn to you inevitably
As the needle to the pole
Turns – as the cold brain to the soul
Turns in its uncertainty:
So I turn and long for you;
So I long for you, and turn
To the love that through my chaos
Burns a truth,
And lights my path.

(c. 1948)

To Live at All Is Miracle Enough

To live at all is miracle enough.
The doom of nations is another thing.
Here in my hammering blood-pulse is my proof.

Let every painter paint and poet sing
And all the sons of music ply their trade;
Machines are weaker than a beetle's wing.

Swung out of sunlight into cosmic shade,
Come what come may the imagination's heart
Is constellation high and can't be weighed.

Nor greed nor fear can tear our faith apart
When every heart-beat hammers out the proof
That life itself is miracle enough.

(c. 1949)

The Old Grey Donkey

The old grey donkey crops the grass and clover
It has moved out of the hot sun into the shade of some laurels.
There are only three sounds in the air, beside the intermittent
                       songs of a few birds –
The first sound is the short sharp grassy note as the donkey's feet
                       stamp forward from time to time
The second is the sound of the grass being torn up by the old
                       whitish mouth
And the third is the sound, as of an army on the march,
When it is moving with precision but with an uncanny slowness
The steady endless munching that gives a slow rhythm to the
                       afternoon.

(1949)

As the Kite that Soars

As the kite that soars on the pull of its line
My heart soars up at the pull of thine
And thine at the pull of mine.

(1949)

Poem

I

What panther stalks tonight as through these London
Groves of iron stalks the strawberry blonde?
Strung through the darkness each electric moon
Throbs like a wound.

II

She tinkles tombwards to the lilt of coins
Down avenues of globe-stars: as she prowls
On heels like stilts, those castanets of doom
Waken the ghouls.

III

Threading the lights and shades, her kerbcraft shames
The ingenious leopard, but her legacy
Of love is dangerous as is the goose-flesh-
Surfaced sea,

IV

For now the inverted tombstone of a starched
And ghastly shirtfront shines like wax beneath
A lamp as something sidles to exchange
A blade for breath.

Where Swallow Street and Piccadilly join
It moves through half light with a slithering sound
And leaves a penknife in the seeded heart
Of the strawberry blonde.

(c. 1950)

The Rebels

By devious paths the rebels make
Their way to centres of revolt
And nests of insurrection shake
With wings in cities half asleep.

From tired homes with burning heads
They stumble into days of mist:
Snapped is their childhood's anchor-chain,
The helm shakes, and a tide is running.

The time for solitary journeys
Among minds. The time for anger.
Suddenly the natural rebel
Finds himself among the firebrands.

Received, he lifts his head, and finds,
In some dark centre of revolt,
He is more lonely among pards
Than when he cursed his parents' love.

(c. 1950)

Poem

With power supernal dowered
The eagle whacks its way
Up streets of gale.
The tiger, sinew-powered,
Tears at the dappled prey
Its claws impale.

Through waters opalescent
The wavering squid proceeds
To sunless hunting-grounds.
Thwarted at the senescent
Moon the jaguar speeds
Among the mounds.

The humming-bird, suspended
Above the bloom, its wings
Invisible, sucks.
A wounded snake has wended
To water that makes rings
While its cold throat works.

I have nor scale, nor pinion,
Nor limbs with thews of steel,
Nor head of gold.
But my imagination
Is tropical and real
As the pen I hold.

(c. 1950)

And Then I Heard Her Speak

And then I heard her speak
And her shrill voice shattered
The alabaster of her brow's
Rare symmetry:
And her loveliness seemed to crumble, and break,
And nothing mattered –
Though I had seen her head turn suddenly
Like a naiad's – and then, her voice:
And the magic was scattered.

Yet now, I find in me
That it has been resolved,
This discord, for an edged
And more fantastic beauty has evolved
As when a shark's fin rips the satin sea.

(c. 1950)

The Flight

While watching the sun sink
Bleeding like Duncan: while marvelling
At the imagination's brink
Upon this thing –

This going down of a murdered
And soundless star,
My mind sped
Suddenly far

From me; it ceased to be mine,
It fled
Like a spirit over the rim of my brain
To a zone of the dead

Where the Murdered-
In-Legends lie
With their dazzling wounds that burn and bleed
Through history.

(c. 1950)

As I Watched between Two Forests

As I watched between two forests
In the dead of night
All in the dire moonlight
I saw a doe come mincing
With high uneasy tread
And sensitive, tense head
Come mincing from the forest
The forest on my right
And cross the glade between,
The moonlight glade of green,
And pass, and pass
Into the left-hand forest
And vanish from my sight.

(c. 1954)

Heads Float about Me

Heads float about me; come and go, absorb me;
Terrify me that they deny the nightmare
That they should be, defy me:
And all the secrecy; the horror
Of truth, of this intrinsic Truth

Drifting, ah God, along the corridors
Of the world: hearing the metal
Clang; and the rolling wheels.
Heads float about me – haunted
By solitary sorrows.

(c. March–August 1958)

Swallow the Sky

Swallow the sky: chew up the stars
And munch the wind
For it's on fire with indigestible glory.
The wild pips of the globe bring, in the end
Nothing but torture, but gorge on, my friend,
Swallow the moon, that hump-backed thing,
Your story...

Your story and the story of the world
The dread of the cold Universe itself
Sings in the heart-bone high:
Gulp the wild globe and spit it out again
Breaking apart the image of your pain
Swallow the sky!

(c. March–August 1958)

Coarse as the Sun Is Blatant

Coarse as the sun is blatant, the high spinach-
Coloured elms, the lawns a yellow matting
Of tired grass, disgust me, and the netting
Of summer boughs that creak at every touch

Of this hot breeze distract me; live apart,
And bring no love to me from other lands,
From other countries, other fields: my hands
Are empty as my blind lob-sided heart!

Lob-sided, for self pity like a curse
Turns all I see to ugliness: the lawns
A wilderness for lack of unicorns,
The elm a tower for birds of paradise.

Nature! I hate you for you scorch my brain
And make me see my weakness yet again.

(c. March–August 1958)

Through the Voluminous Foliage of the Mind

Through the voluminous foliage of the mind
The green thoughts float from branch to branch or wind
In airy gyres through the sentient leaves.
I know that there is nothing they can find
Beyond the teeming trail that beauty leaves,
The grievous trail, invisible O! god:
I only see where glory's feet have strayed.

(c. March–August 1958)

On Fishing Up a Marble Head

What is it then that has so swathed your face?
Have time and water blurred you to a boulder?
There's no trace
Of clinging gauze or sea-mist to bewilder,
Nor has my sight
Lost focus. Can it be the blue
And tireless fingers of the tides of night
Have soothed away what once was chiselled new?

I hold you in my hands. The beams pour down
Athwart the glistening of your lids and crown,
Pour where the waters poured. O heavy head
Worn to the will of the sub-aqueous dead.
Now is your hour to draw your breath; but O
How can I let you go?
Yet hold you so?

(c. March–August 1958)

Poem

That lance of light that slid across the dark
To disappear a moment later, when
A cloud like a great haystack with its angry
Hair awry devoured it and then spat
It out like the barbed war-head of a lyric,
Sang earthward, and a million light-years later
Pierced the green dark of a tall weed-hung vessel,
And in a cup of honey-coloured light
Hissed at the impact.

(c. March–August 1958)

Poem

When I was wounded
I walked alone:
It was not deep
But the voice began,

Of an old, cold Lady
Who called me and said –
'Here is my bosom
To rest your head.'

'Old, cold Lady –'
I said to her,
'I know of bosoms
Softer far
To sleep upon.'

The old, cold Lady
Turned away.
'I had forgotten –'
I heard her say,
'How old I am... how old I am...'

(c. March–August 1958)

Poem

Out of the overlapping
Leaves of my brain came tapping...
Tapping... a voice that is not mine alone:
Nor can the woodpecker
Claim it as his: the flicker
Deep in the foliage belongs to neither
Birds, men, or dreams.

It is as far away as childhood seems.

(c. March–August 1958)

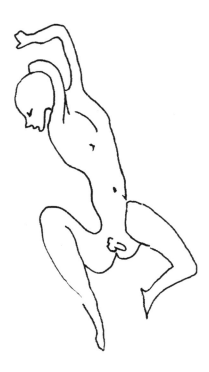

Poem

As though it were not his, he throws his body
Across the sands, the wiry boy from no-where
With his hair in his eyes:
Unwittingly he rides the sandy air,
And with each bound he tears away whatever
It is that holds together
The spirit and the clay: his passion throws
His limbs across a sky of darkening rose.

(c. March–August 1958)

Break Through Naked

Break through naked!
Break through bloody!
Break through Child!

As the fire
Breaks the mountain
And the living
Limbs of lava
Lace the world
While the atom
Casts its shadow
Round the terror
Sated planet
And the continents
Of gooseflesh
Bare their bosoms
To the wild

Break through naked!
Break through bloody!
Break through Child!

(c. March–August 1958)

Poem

Thunder the Christ of it. The field is free:
To everyone his choice: that martial fellow,
His mouth cram full of nails squats in a tree:
Gallop you traitors in. Judas in yellow:

While bibles burn, Leviticus and all,
Christ is forgotten in a world of wit:
Soak up the planets in a swab of gall,
This is the day and we must pay for it.

(c. 1958)

Hail! Tommy-Two-Legs

Hail! Tommy-two-legs, gobbler that you are,
Muncher of herds; swiller of lake and stream.
Are you still hungry, thirsty, suicidal?
Or is it all a dream?

What of the birds that have no tale to tell?
They stand upon their slender sticks and cry,
Hail Mr Cleversticks, the world is waiting
To watch you saunter by.

(c. 1958)

Great Hulk down the Astonished Waters Drifting

Great hulk down the astonished waters drifting:
Hulk of green crust the ocean birds disdain:
I hear her mutter that the pain is shifting.

See where the dolphins shall not sport again:
There drifts the hulk: the seaweed round her throat
A dripping necklace thicker than a mane

And cold as loneliness. She is afloat
On heavy water, wallowing like those
That rock themselves for comfort in remote

Corners of wards, or, when the anguish grows,
Curl up like hedgehogs when the light is raw.
Great hulk of love, how thick the water flows...

Where is her captain and the famous shore
Where danced the golden sailors? Where's the sea
That sang of water when the heart was free
And mermaids swam where mermaids swim no more?

(c. 1958)

For Maeve

Now, with the rain about her, I can see
This is her climate. O my aqueous one
How you do scorn the bright beams of the sun!
How you do drink the wet beams of the sky!

Her head is glimmering in the slanting strands.
It is her climate for the storm is making:
While others bask, she wanders to her slaking.
How rare she is, her brow, her breast, her hands.

(July 1960)

224

Undated Poems

An Armful of Roses

I turned to look again, and as I turned
She turned a little also, so that something burned,
Something of fire that mixed itself with snow
In a great whorl of exquisite heat and cold.
But where in all that riot, where was she?
Why did *she* hide and go?

Which was her face among that storm of roses?
Looped in her circling arm,
O indivisible,
It turned among the petals half astray
Into another clime; another day,
And she was gone away,
An eyelid lifting as a rosebud closes.

I Cross the Narrow Bridges to Her Love

I cross the narrow bridges to her love
The brittle bridges and the angry fords:
Beneath the quick, white river, and above
The white page of the sky with clouds like words.

Deployed in fretted columns; see them moving,
Deployed along the river. Where is she
Who waits for love to come to her sweet breast
As I desire it? – but the brittle bridges
And the little fords that I must cross, or wade,
Are tortuous, and make my heart afraid.

My Malady Is This

My malady is this
That agony and bliss
Are indivisibly
Woven in me.

Ah! How melodiously
The death-bird cries in me –
How anguished the lorn kiss
Of loveliness.

At Such an Hour as This

At such an hour as this, the night being silent
And starless, and my room being lightless
And the fire being nothing but ashes
And my being alone in the house with the latches
Down and the curtains almost drawn
I fell asleep and awoke at last in the dawn
And knew I had spent the night well in company
With the ghost of me

Staring in Madness

Search the steep midnight of the forest wall
And you will sense a green-ness in the black.
Stare into this green midnight till the call
Of a small crow draws seven thorned branches back.

Then will a hollow ride cathedral-cold
Of giant laurel be unfolded, and
You will observe a child of steel and gold
Approaching with a phial in its hand.

O then, close up your eyes, and seal them lightly
With a great wall for blindness; it may be
You have not known the gold of love, nor [rightly]
Have felt the tempered steel of enmity.

For God's Sake Draw the Blind

For God's sake draw the blind and shut away
The beauty that is crowding through the window
A scene of rain-drenched elms and four drenched pastures,
All apple green against the leaden sky.
I do not want it – I am out of tune
With all this lushness. To hell with it.
Draw the thick blinds; put on the light.
I will not watch the green leaves fluttering on the dark,
I will not watch it. I am far too tired
Of the responsibility for miracles.
O vulnerable when nature cries to them
And lifts the corner of her common veil...

A Presage of Death

A shadow wades over the earth, over the long earth and approaches me, climbs my clay and engulfs me until I am older than fear and have no age, but am standing lonely in an ancient cold, for I have been swarmed by death, and though I hear as though through a veil of ice the shrill electric notes of a bird entering at my dead ears, yet neither I nor the bird are of the world any longer, or if the bird still lives, then it is that I am hearing its voice across the dynasties, from the maw of a cold to-morrow. My hand moves on its own earth in lamplight and I am rehearsing my certain death! A black rehearsal in an evening field.
'What sound is that?' 'It is the sound of silence, for the bird has ended its remote singing.'
O Sunlight! Sunlight! Mock me no longer with that yellow dusk. Oh wither up you chill and sudden truth, and let me have forgetful song again.

The Eclipse

Who beat the little gong at the eclipse?
We do not know who beat the little gong!
Who struck apart those old and brassy lips
So that they froze all China with a groan
And did our people wrong?

Who shocked the sacred emperor, who lay
Naked in homage on his lawn,
                              (The ships
Stood in their moorings spellbound)
                                        Wilt thou say!
Who beat the little gong at the eclipse?

Lies! Lies! It Is All Lies and Nothing Else

Lies! lies! it is all lies and nothing else,
This illness of deceit, this self-pretence
Of *being*: I am digging for myself
In word and act each hour a dirty grave
In which to shovel my astounded heart
Which longs for light, which hourly longs for light
The while my crass brain treads the death-marl in
While what is greater, struggles. More than I!
Oh, how much more than I, you fabulous thing
I so incarcerate! For I do hold
Health in my poisoned prison. No, not I
You are, but more, yet cannot spread your white
And earthless wings aflame with luna-light
In the cramped compass of my sexton's head.
Yet only are they strong through cause of me –
If not of me, there would be no such plumes
To so belittle me with fitful radiance
And were my skull no gaol, where'd be the wings
To scorn my self deceit, or point the lie,
The fever and the darkness that is I –

Love Is an Angry Weather

Love is an angry weather, love is torn
With the italic lightnings, but love is also
Of the square script of silent mountains born,
And of the dazzling zones of timeless snow,
O limitless as paper under the faltering
Nib; and violent as the many pointed
Oath of a spattered ink star shattering
Joy's oracle, O Love, thou blackly printed
Midnight-gulping, twilight-straying,
Sweet, noon-fruited, dawn-fantastic
Living Legend, greedy and gold-flinging,
Brittle as lampglass and elastic
As naked sapling from the white dew springing.

O Love, the Steeplejack

O love, the steeplejack, can climb
The high fanes of the cheekbones steep,
And in the belfry of cold ducts
Can pull the bell-tears down.
O love! dismantling love, the time
By the dark clock in the brow is deep
In midnight. Pull the midnight down
And wake the sunbeam.

She Lies in Candlelight

She lies in candlelight upon
A bed, like a dim galleon
That o'er the carpet journeys on,

In silence through the candled gloom
And yet remains in this small room –
A ghost-ship with a golden bloom

Of golden hair, that deepens now
In shadow at the galleon's prow
As on the seas of time they flow.

Than Paper and a Pen

Than paper and a pen
What is there, then,
Needed besides
To make the cold ink burn?
Only a leaping brain;
Only the heart's hot tides;
Only the frond of a fern

In the skull for a feeler,
Touching on pain –
(Neither hurter nor healer)
Touching on joy –
(Nor for love nor for gain)
Touching on all
For its singular stain.

Notes

For a full account of the poems' publication history see the *Peake Studies* website, peakestudies.com/contents.htm, 'A Title and First-Line Index to Peake's Poems', compiled by G. Peter Winnington.

p. 21 'Birth of Day': unpublished. Source: letter to Gordon Smith dated 1929. Full stops added at end of first two stanzas.
p. 21 'Vikings': f.p. in *Cassell's Magazine* (March 1932), p. 59. Date: f.p.
p. 22 'Coloured Money': f.p. in *LM*, vol. 36, no. 214 (August 1937), p. 325. Reprinted, revised, in *S&S*, pp. 22–3. Date written on TS in Peake's hand.
p. 23 'If I Could See, Not Surfaces': f.p. as 'Overture' in *LM*, vol. 39, no.

139 (January 1939), pp. 285–6. Reprinted, revised, in *S&S*, pp. 17–18. Date written on TS in Peake's hand.

p. 25 'Palais de Danse': f.p. in *S&S*, pp. 7–8. Date written on TS in Peake's hand. A MS dates it 1939.

p. 27 'Rhondda Valley': f.p. in *LM*, vol. 36, no. 216 (October 1937), pp. 507–9. Reprinted, revised, in *S&S*, pp. 2–4. Date that of Peake's only visit to Wales.

p. 30 'Heaven Hires Me': f.p. in *10P* as 'Heaven Lures Me'. Source: MS. A full stop has been added at line 11, 'of' at line 16. Date that of Peake's only visit to Wales (see line 23).

p. 31 'The Metal Bird': f.p. in *LM*, vol. 36, no. 214 (August 1937), pp. 325–6. Date that of Peake's only visit to Wales (see line 2).

p. 31 'The Cocky Walkers': f.p. in *NEW* (27 May 1937), p. 130. Reprinted in *S&S*, p. 2. Date written on TS in Peake's hand, where the title is 'Battersea'.

p. 33 'Poplar': f.p. in *NEW* (13 May 1937), p. 90. Date: f.p.

p. 33 'These Eyes Have Noosed a Hundred Hills': unpublished. Source: Bod. Dep. Peake 9, fol. 38b^r (MS). Date: an earlier draft of the poem on the same page identifies the scene as Austria, which Peake visited in 1937 (see *VA*, p. 101).

p. 34 'Mané Katz': unpublished. Source: N1, p. 38. Date given in poem.

p. 35 'Two Seasons': f.p. as 'Autumn: I stretched the shrilly limbs at cuckoo-time' in *NEW* (14 July 1938), p. 260. Reprinted, revised, in *S&S*, p. 8. I have dated the poem to the November before f.p.

p. 36 'Autumn: The lit mosaic of the wood': f.p. in *NEW* (6 January 1938), p. 250, which is my source. Here line 16 reads: 'At the turn of turn of the road'; this is corrected in N2, p. 71. I have dated the poem to the Autumn before f.p.

p. 37 'The Crystal': f.p. in *NEW* (23 September 1937), p. 390. Date: f.p.

p. 38 'To Maeve: You walk unaware': f.p. in *S&S*, as dedication. Date: Walter de la Mare saw this poem in 1937, and invited Maeve and Mervyn to his house on the strength of it 'just before we were married' (see *AWA*, pp. 29–30).

p. 39 'Poem: Body and head and arms and throat and hands': f.p. as 'The Meeting at Dawn' in *NEW* (30 December 1937), p. 230. Reprinted as 'Poem', *S&S*, p. 21. Date: f.p.

p. 39 'How Foreign to the Spirit's Early Beauty': f.p. in *RoB*, p. 30. Source: N2, p. 27. The word 'curve' in line 3 is unclear in the MS. Date suggested in *AWA*, p. 25.

p. 40 'Sing I the Fickle, Fit-for-Nothing Fellows': f.p. in *L*, vol. 18, no. 464 (1 December 1937), p. 1206. Reprinted in *Gb*, p. 13. Date: f.p.

p. 41 'El Greco': f.p. in *NEW* (9 June 1938), p. 170. Reprinted, revised, in *RoB*, p. 27. The version I give is from N2, p. 19 (TS amended in Peake's hand). Date given in N1, p. 32.

p. 41 'Spring': f.p. in *NEW* (26 May 1938), p. 130. Date: f.p.

p. 42 'Watch, Here and Now…': f.p. in *Pinpoints*, no. 4 (May–June 1939), p. 25. Date is that of Peake's visit to Paris in 1938; see *VA*, p. 109.

p. 43 'Au Moulin Joyeux': f.p. in *Eve's Journal* (July 1939), p. 48. Date given in poem.

p. 44 'Van Gogh': f.p. in *S&S*, p. 19. Date given in *PP*, p. 245.

p. 44 'I, While the Gods Laugh, the World's Vortex Am': f.p. in *NEW* (20 April 1939), p. 8. Reprinted in *S&S*, pp. 9–10. Date: f.p.

p. 45 'Epstein's Adam': f.p. in *Picture Post*, vol. 4, no. 4 (29 July 1939), p. 67. Written in support of Epstein's statue of Adam, which caused a public outcry when displayed at the Leicester Galleries in June 1939 (see *VA*, p. 114). Date: f.p.

p. 46 'Burgled Beauty': f.p. in *Eve's Journal* (August 1939), p. 63. Date: f.p.

p. 47 'September 1939': unpublished. Source: N2, p. 55 (MS). Date given in poem.

p. 48 'We Are the Haunted People': f.p. in *RoB*, p. 5. Source: N1, p. 41. Date given in *AWA*, pp. 34–5.

p. 49 'She Whose Body Was in Pain': f.p. in *RoB*, p. 10. Source: N1, unpaginated section. Date is that of Peake's mother's death.

p. 50 'Now Are Gathering in the Skies': unpublished. Source: N1, unpaginated section. Date is that of Peake's mother's death.

p. 50 'Where Skidded Only in the Upper Air': f.p. in *L* vol. 22, no. 564 (2 November 1939), p. 848. Date: f.p.

p. 51 'The Boy': f.p. in *RoB*, p. 22. Source: N2, p. 22. Date given in *PP*, p. 166.

p. 52 'The World': f.p. in *11P*. Source: N1, p. 1. Dash added at end of first stanza. Date that of N1.

p. 52 'The Women of the World Inhabit Her': f.p. in *11P*. Source: N1, p. 5. Full stop added at end. Date that of N1.

p. 52 'O Heart-Beats': f.p. in *10P*. Source: N1, p. 6. Full stop added at end. Date that of N1.

p. 53 'Sensitive Head': unpublished. Source: N1, p. 7. Date that of N1.

p. 54 'The Sands Were Frosty When the Soul Appeared': unpublished. Source: N1, p. 8. Date that of N1.

p. 54 'I Could Sit Here an Age-Long of Green Light': f.p. in *12P*. Source: N1, p. 9. Full stop added at end. Date that of N1.

p. 55 'Dreams': f.p. in *11P*. Source: N1, p. 10. Date that of N1.

p. 56 'Where Got I These Two Eyes that Plunder Storm': f.p. in *12P*. Source: N1, p. 11. Date that of N1.

p. 57 'I, Like an Insect on the Stainéd Glass': unpublished. Source: N1, 12. Full stop added at end. Date that of N1.

p. 57 'Swung through Dead Aeons': f.p. in *11P*. Source: N1, p. 13. Date that of N1.

p. 58 'Autumn: There is a surge of stillness bred': f.p. in *RoB*, p. 29. Source: N1, p. 14. Date that of N1.

p. 59 'Eagle': f.p. in *RoB*, p. 21, where 'Sheers' in the first line is 'Sneers'. Source: N1, p. 15. Full stop added at end. Date that of N1.

p. 60 'The Sap of Sorrow Mounts This Rootless Tree': f.p. in *11P*. Source: N1, p. 16. Date that of N1.

p. 60 'Moon': f.p. in *10P*. Source: N1, p. 17. Date that of N1.

p. 61 'No Creed Shall Bind Me to a Sapless Bole': f.p. in *10P*. Source: N1, pp. 18–19. Comma added at line 6 and question mark at line 18. Date that of N1.

p. 62 'As Over the Embankment': f.p. in *10P*. Source: N1, p. 20. Date that of N1.

p. 63 'Blake': f.p. in *RoB*, p. 24. Source: N1, p. 21. Comma added at end of first stanza. Date that of N1.

p. 63 'Fame Is My Tawdry Goal': f.p. in *12P*. Source: N1, p. 22. Date that of N1.

p. 64 'Often, in the Evenings': f.p. in *10P*. Source: N1, p. 23. Date that of N1.

p. 65 'I Am Almost Drunken': unpublished; quoted in *MEMG*, pp. 224–5. Source: N1, p. 24. Date that of N1.

p. 65 'Balance': f.p. (as 'In Crazy Balance') in *SP*, p. 9. Source: N1, p. 25. Full stop added at end. Date that of source.

p. 66 'The Torch': unpublished. Source: N1, p. 28. Date that of N1.

p. 66 'Stand with Me': unpublished. Source: N1, p. 29. Full stop added at end. Date that of N1.

p. 67 'I Sing a Hatred of the Black Machine': unpublished. Source: N1, pp. 30–2. Full stop added at line 30 and at the end. Date that of N1.

p. 68 'Lit, Every Stage': unpublished. Source: N1; inserted between pp. 32 and 33. Full stop added at line 11 and at the end. Date that of N1.

p. 69 'She Does Not Know': unpublished. Source: N1, p. 33. Full stop added at end of first stanza. The 'miller's son' is Rembrandt. Date that of N1.

p. 70 'Life Beat Another Rhythm': unpublished; quoted in *MEMG*, p. 83. Source: N1, p. 34. Full stop added at line 2. Date that of N1.

p. 70 'Oh Sprightly and Lightly': unpublished. Source: N1, p. 35. Full stops added at lines 2 and 7; dash at line 9. Date that of N1.

p. 71 'What Is That against the Sky?': unpublished. Source: N1, p. 36. Date that of N1.

p. 71 'Oh I Must End This War within My Heart': unpublished. Source: N1, p. 36. Date that of N1.

p. 72 'Beauty, What Are You?': unpublished. Source: N1, p. 37. Full stops added at end of first and second stanzas. Date that of N1.

p. 73 'The Modelles': f.p. in *SP*, p. 37. Source: N1, p. 39. Date that of N1.

p. 73 'I Found Myself Walking': unpublished. Source: N1, inserted between pp. 39 and 40. Full stop added at end of first stanza, question mark at end of second. Date that of N1.

p. 74 'Along with Everything Else': unpublished. Source: N1, p. 43. Date that of N1.

p. 74 'Am I to Say Goodbye to Trees and Leaves?': unpublished. Source: N1, pp. 44–5. Question mark added at line 13. Date that of N1.

p. 75 'To All Things Solid as to All Things Flat': unpublished. Source: N1, unpaginated section. Date that of N1.

p. 75 'When God Had Pared His Fingernails': f.p. in *RoB*, p. 20. Source: N1, unpaginated section. Full stop added at line 7; comma added at line 10. Date that of N1.

p. 76 'For All Your Deadly Implications': unpublished. Source: N1, unpaginated section. Date that of N1.

p. 76 'O She Has Walked All Lands There Are': unpublished. Source: N1, unpaginated section. Full stops added at lines 4 and 8. Date that of N1.

p. 77 'Grottoed beneath Your Ribs Our Babe Lay Thriving': f.p. in *First Time in America* (1948), pp. 133–4. Reprinted in *Gb*, pp. 4–5. Date that of the birth of Peake's first son, Sebastian.

p. 79 'In the Fabric of This Love': f.p. in *RoB*, p. 8, where date is given. Source: N2, p. 2.

p. 79 'May 1940': f.p. in *RoB*, p. 3. Source: N2, p. 25 (TS). Question mark added at line 10. Date given in title.

p. 80 'Troop Train': f.p. in *MEMG*, p. 95, where date is suggested. Source: N2, p. 53, where it is titled 'Conscript'; but in a list of poems in Peake's hand given later in N2 it is titled 'Troop Train', as in *MEMG*.

p. 80 'Fort Darland': f.p. in *RoB*, p. 2. Source: N2, p. 22 (TS). The date is that of Peake's basic training at Fort Darland.

p. 81 'In the Lion's Yellow Eyes': f.p. and source: Smith, p. 78. Date: Peake saw the lion in Blackpool in October and sent the poem to Smith in mid-November.

p. 82 'Every Gesture Every Eyelid's': unpublished. Source: UCL Box I (ii), fol. 63ᵛ. Full stop added at end. Date: the dates given indicate the period covered by the source.

p. 82 'Leave Train': f.p. in *MEMG*, p. 107. Source: N2, p. 50. Date conjectural; Peake was in Blackpool in November 1940.

p. 83 'The Shapes': f.p. in *Poems from the Forces* (1941), pp. 85–6. Reprinted, revised, in *S&S*, pp. 13–14. Dated 1940 in *PP*, p. 161; the bombing of Coventry mentioned at line 51 took place on 14 November 1940.

p. 85 'To a Scarecrow Gunner': unpublished. Source: UCL Box I (iii), fol. 128ᵛ. Full stops added at lines 8, 9 and 14. Date: the dates given indicate the period covered by the source.

p. 85 'From the Hot Chaos of the Many Habitations': unpublished. Source: UCL Box I (iii), fol. 128aʳ. Date: the dates given indicate the period covered by the source.

p. 86 'Rather than a Little Pain': f.p. in *S&S*, pp. 18–19. Date given in *PP*, p. 253.

p. 86 'The Two Fraternities': f.p. in *S*, vol. 167 (8 August 1941), p. 130. Reprinted in *S&S*, p. 8. Date given in *PP*, p. 251.

p. 87 'With People, So with Trees': f.p. in *Gb*, p. 24. Date given in *PP*, p. 255.

p. 87 'Onetime my Notes Would Dance': f.p. in *SP*, p. 33. Source: Bod. Dep. Peake 10, fol. 3ʳ (MS). Date: on the reverse of the MS there is a sketch plan of *Titus Groan*, chs 14–18. Peake was working on these chapters in 1940.

p. 88 'London, 1941': f.p. in *S*, vol. 167 (12 December 1941), p. 555. Reprinted in *S&S*, p. 1. Date: on 7 February 1941 Peake was working on a painting 'dominated by a personification of "London" in the form of a brick and mortar figure of a woman holding a child… half human, half masonry' (unpublished letter). The resemblance of the painting to the poem suggests that he may have written the poem at about this time.

p. 89 'The Sullen Accents Told of Doom': unpublished. Source: UCL Box 1 (iv), fol. 37ʳ. Date: the MS is dated 1941; for month see poem.

p. 90 'Before Man's Bravery I Bow My Head': f.p. as 'The Time Has Come for More Than Small Decisions' in *RoB*, p. 4, where date is given. Source: N2, p. 9. Full stop added at line 6.

p. 90 'The Spadesmen': f.p. in *S*, vol. 167 (25 July 1941), p. 81. Reprinted, revised, in *S&S*, p. 10. Date: f.p.

p. 91 'The Craters': f.p. in *Now*, no. 7 (Fall 1941), p. 24. Reprinted in *S&S*, p. 6. Date: f.p.

p. 93 'They Move with Me, My War-Ghosts': f.p. in *S&S*, pp. 5–6. Date: f.p.

p. 95 'Had Each a Voice, What Would His Fingers Cry': f.p. in *Poems from the Forces* (1941), p. 87. Reprinted in *S&S*, p. 9. Date: f.p.

p. 95 'What Is It Muffles the Ascending Moment?': f.p. in *S&S*, pp. 10–11. Date: f.p.

p. 96 'I Am For Ever with Me': f.p. in *S&S*, pp. 11–13. Date: f.p.

p. 99 'The Sounds': f.p. in *S&S*, pp. 14–16. Date: f.p.

p. 101 'The Colt': f.p. in *S&S*, p. 19. Date: f.p.

p. 102 'The Burning Boy': f.p. in *S&S*, p. 20. Date: f.p.

p. 103 'Is There No Love Can Link Us?': f.p. in *S&S*, p. 21. Date: f.p.

p. 103 'Swan Arrogant': f.p. in *S&S*, pp. 21–2. Date : f.p.

p. 104 'London Buses': f.p. in *12P*. Source: N2, p. 17 (TS). Date given in N2.

p. 106 'A Reverie of Bone': f.p. in *3AQ*, no. 3 (Autumn 1960), pp. 22–31. Reprinted in *RoB*, pp. 11–18. Date given as 1941 in *PP*, p. 257; but Smith (p. 100) says Peake worked on the poem for a decade or so: 'He used to read me extracts over a period that must have spanned ten years'. An early draft of the first two stanzas appears in UCL Box 2 (vi) (a notebook he began in September 1941), fol. 61ʳ. My own view is that the poem was substantially composed at Larkhill in Wiltshire, where Peake was stationed between December 1941 and March 1942. I base this conjecture on the evidence provided by Bod. Dep. Peake 7, an exercise book labelled 'Peake, Larkhill', which contains a complete MS version of 'A Reverie of Bone' entitled 'Valley of Bones' (fols. 9ʳ–17ʳ). I have used this MS as my source, comparing it with the annotated TS in Bod. Dep. Peake 9, fols. 118ʳ–132ʳ, which was clearly prepared from the MS. Both MS and TS include seven stanzas that have been scored out in the TS – not necessarily by Peake – and do not appear in any printed version. These are stanzas 10, 15, 19, 23, 29, 37 and 43. In both, too, the first stanza is not repeated at the end. My reason for restoring the missing stanzas is that without them the poem does not seem to me to make sense. I think too that the punctuation of the MS – which I have mostly followed, though I have sometimes accepted alternatives from the TS – clarifies the poem's meaning. I kept the repetition of the first stanza at the end for no better reason than that it seemed to me effective. I have also retained one line from the printed versions for lack of anything better: this is the last line of stanza 42, 'Scudding across the melancholy land'. In the MS this line is 'And yet, before the evening, some bleak breeze', and 'Scudding across the melancholy land' is the first line of what would have been stanza 43; but since Peake never completed this stanza I have left stanza 42 as it is in the printed versions. I have added commas at lines 2 and 5 of stanza 12; and a dash at the end of stanza 19. Comma omitted at the end of stanza 42, line 4.

p. 116 'Suddenly, Walking along the Open Road': f.p. in *SP*, p. 36. Source: Bod. Dep. Peake 10, fol. 8ʳ (MS). Date conjectural, based on reference to Wiltshire, where Peake was stationed at Larkhill from December 1941 to March 1942.

p. 117 'They Loom Enormous': unpublished. Source: Bod. Dep. Peake 7, fol. 18ʳ (MS). Date that of source (a notebook labelled 'Larkhill'; see note to 'A Reverie of Bone', above).

p. 117 'Maeve': f.p. in *MEMG*, p. 107. Source: N2, p. 15. *MEMG* prints an additional line at the end, 'Can you not quieten this climbing wave', but the source shows that this was intended as an alternative to the one given, not an addition to it. Date given in N2.

p. 118 'What Can I Ever Offer You': unpublished. Source: UCL Box 2 (vi), fol. 71ᵛ. Question mark added at end of first stanza. Date: the first date given in Box 2 (vi) is September 1941. The poem was presumably written shortly before the birth of Peake's second son, Fabian, on 2 April 1942.

p. 118 'O, This Estrangement Forms a Distance Vaster': f.p. in *Poetry Quarterly*, vol. 10, no. 1 (Spring 1948), p. 4. Reprinted, revised, in *Gb*, p. 10. Date: Maeve Gilmore suggests that he wrote this around the time of Fabian's birth (*AWA*, p. 46).

p. 119 'An April Radiance of White Light Dances': f.p. in *Gb*, p. 36. There is an earlier version in N2, p. 51. Date suggested in *VA*, pp. 202–3.

p. 119 'May 1942': unpublished. Source: UCL Box 2 (vii), fol. 12ᵛ. Date given in title.

p. 120 'Blue as the Indigo and Fabulous Storm': unpublished. Source: TS. A gap in the TS indicates that a word may be missing before 'brilliance' at line 17, and in the same line the word 'past' is given as 'part'. I have added dashes at line 16 and a full stop at the end of the poem. Date: the poem was clearly written while Peake was undergoing treatment for 'neurosis' at the Southport Emergency Hospital, from May to September 1942, where patients were issued with 'shapeless "suits" of peacock blue with crimson rag ties', as Peake put it in a letter to Gordon Smith (Smith, p. 86).

p. 121 'Curl Up in the Great Window Seat': unpublished. Source: UCL MS Add. 234, Box 2 (vii), back cover. The cover is marbled, which makes the poem difficult to read; but Peake lists it as publishable at the end of N2 (unpaginated section). Date: the dates given indicate the period covered by the source.

p. 121 'Digging a Trench I Found a Heart-Shaped Stone': f.p. in *Gb*, p. 8. Date given in *PP*, p. 165.

p. 122 'Absent from You Where Is There Corn and Wine?': f.p. in *Gb*, p. 37. Date given in *PP*, p. 564.

p. 123 'I am the Slung Stone that No Target Has': unpublished. Source: N2, p. 44. Full stop added at lines 2 and 13. Date implied by poem (in line 2, 'Thirty one summers' has been struck out).

p. 123 'If I would stay what men call sane': unpublished. Source: UCL Box 2 (ix), fol. 54ᵛ. The date given is that of source.

p. 124 'Poem: Taller than life, deployed along the shallows': f.p. in *12P*. Source: Bod. Dep. Peake 10, fol. 6ʳ (MS). Date given in Dep. Peake 9, fol. 8ʳ (TS).

p. 125 'The Glassblowers': f.p. in *Gb*, pp. 19–20. Date is that of Peake's time working for the Ministry of Information on drawings and paintings of Birmingham glass-blowers; see *VA*, pp. 161–3, and *MEMG*, pp. 116–8.

p. 128 'Dead Rat': f.p. in *RoB*, p. 25. Source: N2, p. 24 (TS). Date given in *PP*, p. 167.

p. 129 'For Maeve: You are the maeve of me': f.p. in *Gb*, p. 30. Date given in *PP*, p. 565.

p. 129 'Tides': f.p. in *RoB*, p. 31. Source: N2, p. 65 (TS). Date given in *PP*, p. 566.

p. 130 'Because Last Night My Child Clung to My Neck': f.p. in *P&D*. Source: Bod. Dep. Peake 9, fol. 36ʳ (TS, with MS correction to last two lines). Date given in *PP*, p. 569.

p. 131 'Poem: My arms are rivers heavy with raw flood': f.p. in *Life and Letters*, vol. 56, no. 127 (March 1948), p. 235. Reprinted in *Gb*, p. 25. Date given in *PP*, p. 570.

p. 132 'The Three': f.p. in *PP*, p. 573, where date is given. Source: N2,

p. 3, and TS amended in Peake's hand.

p. 133 'The Consumptive. Belsen 1945': f.p. as 'Belsen 1945' in *Counterpoint*, vol. 2 (1945). Reprinted, revised, as 'The Consumptive – Belsen 1945' in *First Time in America* (1948), pp. 134–5; then with further revisions in *Gb*, p. 15. Date is that of Peake's visit to the concentration camp at Bergen-Belsen.

p. 135 'This German Pinewood': unpublished. Source: N2, p. 32. Date is that of Peake's travels through Germany at the end of the war.

p. 136 'The World is Broken without Love': unpublished. Source: N2, p. 45. Date given in N2.

p. 136 'Yet Who to Love Returning': unpublished. Source: N2, p. 46. There is another version in Bod. Dep. Peake 9, p. 15, from which I have taken the title. Date given in N2.

p. 137 'Victims': f.p. in *3AQ*, no. 2 (Summer 1960), p. 5. Titled 'Bomb Victims' in Bod. Dep. Peake 9, fols. 96^r, 100^r. An early version is in N2, p. 6. Date given in Bod. Dep. Peake 9, fol. 100^r, which is my source.

p. 138 'Poem: Remote, that baleful head of his': f.p. in *12P*. Source: Bod. Dep. Peake 9, fols. 9^r and 10^r (TSS). Date given in source, fol. 10^r.

p. 139 'All Eden Was Then Girdled by My Arms': f.p. in *Phoenix* (Autumn 1946), p. 19. Reprinted, revised, in *Gb*, p. 23. Date: f.p.

p. 139 'The Vastest Things Are Those We May Not Learn': f.p. as 'The Enforced Return' in *Strand*, vol. 112, issue 671 (November 1946), p. 58. Reprinted with new title in *Gb*, p. 14. Date: f.p.

p. 140 'Poem: It is at times of half-light that I find': f.p. as 'If the Earth were Lamplit' in *Strand*, vol. 112, issue 671 (November 1946), p. 58; reprinted with new title in *Gb*, p. 35. Date: f.p.

p. 141 'Each Day We Live Is a Glass Room': f.p. in *Gb*, p. 17. Date: an early version is in N2, p. 4.

p. 141 'As a Great Town Draws the Eccentrics In': f.p. in *New English Review Magazine*, vol. 3, no. 1 (July 1949), p. 42. Reprinted in *Gb*, p. 11. Date: the poem is in N2, p. 5.

p. 143 'Conscious that Greatness Has Its Tinder Here': unpublished. Source: N2, p. 8. Date that of N2.

p. 143 'The Restaurant': unpublished. Source: N2, p. 8 (TS). Dash added at line 10. Date that of N2.

p. 144 'If Trees Gushed Blood': f.p. in *SP*, p. 43. Source: N2, p. 9 (TS). Date that of N2.

p. 144 'When the Heart Cries in Love': unpublished. Source: N2, p. 10. Commas added at lines 1 and 5. Date that of N2.

p. 145 'What Is that Noise in the Shaking Trees?': unpublished. Source: N2, p. 10. Comma added at line 7 and full stop at line 8. Date that of N2.

p. 146 'Neither to Captain nor be Captained, I': f.p. in *12P*. Source: TS, compared with a less coherent version in N2, p. 11. Question mark added at end. Date that of N2.

p. 147 'Crumbles the Crested Scroll': unpublished. Source: N2, p. 11. Date that of N2.

p. 147 'Wayward O World and Unpredictable': unpublished. Source: N2, p. 12. Date that of N2.

p. 147 'O Love, the World's Solution': unpublished. Source: N2, p. 13. Date that of N2.

p. 148 'When Tiger-Men Sat Their Mercurial Coursers': f.p. in *Gb*, p. 22, which is my source. An early version occurs in N2, p. 14 (TS), which suggests the date. This version has a final stanza that invokes the perverse beauty of the Blitz.

p. 149 'This Field Is Dim with Sheaves': unpublished. Source: N2, p. 16. Exclamation mark added at end of first stanza; dash added at line 10. Date that of N2.

p. 149 'Brave Lies Conspiring in the Three-Hued Flag': unpublished. Source: N2, p. 16 (TS). Date that of N2.

p. 150 'Are We Not the Richer?': unpublished. Source: N2, p. 19 (TS). Date that of N2.

p. 151 'The Pit-Boy's Lung Is Black': unpublished. Source: N2, p. 20. Date that of N2.

p. 151 'Crisis': unpublished. Source: N2, p. 23. Full stop added at line 10, comma at the end of line 16. Date that of N2.

p. 152 'It Is the Malady': unpublished. Source: N2, p. 26. Question mark added at end of first stanza. Date that of N2.

p. 152 'At My Inmost Heart Is Fear': unpublished. Source: N2, p. 28. Full stop added at end of first stanza. Date that of N2.

p. 154 'This Is the Darkness': unpublished. Source: N2, p. 30. Date that of N2.

p. 154 'I Cannot Find It in Me to Be Gay': unpublished. Source: N2, p. 30. Full stop added at end of first stanza. Date that of N2.

p. 155 'There Is No Difference between Night and Day': f.p. in *SP*, p. 44. Source: N2, p. 31. A later page of the notebook indicates the poem's title in a list of poems; *SP* gives it as 'No Difference'. Full stop added at end of poem. Date that of N2.

p. 155 'The Heart Holds Memories Older than the Mind's': f.p. in *Gb*, p. 39. Date: there is an early draft in N2, p. 35.

p. 156 'Lug Out Your Spirit from its Cage of Clay': unpublished. Source: N2, p. 36. Punctuation added at lines 2 and 4. Date that of N2.

p. 156 'There Is an Aristocracy of Love': unpublished. Source: N2, p. 37. Date that of N2.

p. 156 'Poem: How dangerous a thing': unpublished. Source: Bod. Dep. Peake 9, fols. 13ʳ and 32ʳ. An earlier version is in N2, p. 39. Date that of N2.

p. 157 'Into the Sky All Men Must Turn Their Eyes': unpublished. Source: N2, p. 40. Date that of N2.

p. 157 'And I Thought You beside Me': f.p. in *RoB*, p. 32. This is a revised version of the last ten lines of an earlier composition, 'Poem: I Watched Where the Tall Trees Shook', published in *S*, vol. 180 (May 21 1948), p. 613. Source: N2, unpaginated section. Date that of N2.

p. 158 'Into the Dusky Well': unpublished. Source: N2, p. 42. Date that of N2.

p. 159 'Satan': f.p. in *SP*, p. 7. Source: Bod. Dep. Peake 10, fol. 1ʳ (MS); also Bod. Dep. Peake 9, fol. 74ʳ (TS). The break between third and fourth couplet is clearly indicated in the TS, not so clearly in the MS. Date: an early draft of the poem occurs in N2, p. 43.

p. 159 'Features Forgo Their Power': f.p. in *Gb*, p. 27. Date: an early draft is in N2, pp. 46–8.

p. 161 'Let Dreams Be Absolute': unpublished. Source: N2, p. 52. Dash added at line 10. The original poem read 'Let dreams be definite', but Peake replaced 'definite' with 'absolute' at lines 1 and 7, and I have presumed he intended to do the same thing at line 12. Date that of N2.

p. 161 'The Birch Saplings': unpublished. Source: N2, p. 54. Comma added at line 1. Date that of N2.

p. 162 'His Head and Hands Were Built for Sin': f.p. in *Gb*, pp. 1–2. Date: an early draft occurs in N2, pp. 56–7.

p. 163 'I Have Become Less Clay than Hazel-Rod': f.p. in *Gb*, p. 32. Date: a draft of the poem occurs in N2, p. 58.

p. 164 'Cold Island! The Splenetic Air': unpublished. Source: N2, p. 59. Date that of N2.

p. 165 'Rembrandt': f.p. in *RoB*, p. 26. Source: N2, p. 60 (TS). Date that of N2.

p. 166 'Victoria Station. 6.58 p.m.': f.p. in *SP*, p. 11. Source: N2, p. 61 (TS). Date that of N2.

p. 166 'Half-Light': unpublished. Source: N2, p. 61 (TS). Date that of N2.

p. 167 'How Shall I Find Me': unpublished. Source: N2, p. 62 (TS). Date that of N2.

p. 167 'Let the Result Be What It May': unpublished. Source: N2, p. 62 (TS). Date that of N2.

p. 168 'Sark; Evening': unpublished. Source: N2, p. 62 (TS). Date that of N2.

p. 168 'That Phoenix Hour': unpublished. Source: N2, p. 64 (TS). Date that of N2.

p. 169 'Robert Frost': f.p. in *SP*, p. 45. Source: N2, p. 64 (TS). Date that of N2.

p. 169 'The Wings': unpublished. Source: N2, p. 65 (TS). Date that of N2.

p. 169 'Written About a Piece of Paper when About to Draw': unpublished. Source: N2, p. 72. Date that of N2.

p. 170 'As Battle Closes In My Body Stoops': unpublished. Source: N2, p. 74. Semi colon added at line 10, full stop at line 11. Date that of N2.

p. 170 'When All Is Said and Done': unpublished. Source: N2, p. 74. Full stop added at end. Date that of N2.

p. 171 'Possessionless, O Leveret': unpublished. Source: N2, p. 76. Full stops added at lines 4, 7, and 13. Date that of N2.

p. 171 'Love So Imperilled Is': unpublished. Source: TS. Quoted in *MEMG*, p. 228. Date: the poem is listed at the end of N2, unpaginated section.

p. 172 'Love's House': unpublished. Source: TS, with the last two lines added in Peake's hand. Date: the poem is listed at the end of N2, unpaginated section.

p. 173 'The Flag Half-Masted Is a People's Poem': unpublished. Source: Bod. Dep. Peake 9, fol. 93ʳ. Full stop added at line 7; 'its ghost' is given as an alternative for 'belief' at line 8. Date: the poem is listed at the end of N2, unpaginated section.

p. 174 'Love, I Had Thought It Rocklike': f.p. in *Gb*, pp. 6–7. Date: the poem is listed at the end of N2, unpaginated section.

p. 176 'Swans Die and a Tower Falls': f.p. in *Gb*, p. 12. Date: the poem is listed at the end of N2, unpaginated section.

p. 177 'And Are You Then Love's Spokesman in the Bone?': f.p. in *Gb*,

p. 26. Date: the poem is listed at the end of N2, unpaginated section.

p. 177 'For Ever through Love's Weather Wandering': unpublished. The title is given in a list of love poems at the end of N2, unpaginated section. Source: undated letter of c. 1946–8. Date that of N2.

p. 178 'The Rhyme of the Flying Bomb': f.p. in 1962; this edition is my source. Early drafts are contained in Bod. Dep. Peake 5, fols. 12ᵛ–13ᵛ, 21ᵛ–32ᵛ. This volume also contains an unpublished section of the poem (fols. 33ᵛ–34ᵛ), 18 stanzas long, in which the sailor begins to tell the story he promised the babe at stanza 49. It concerns an encounter with a merman. The date of the poem is given in *MEMG*, p. 311. The date given in *PP* is 1949 (p. 445), but Watney says it was 'written in Sark just after the war', p. 154, and Gilmore says it was written 'a year or two' after 1945 (*AWA*, p. 52), and that it was completed 'almost in one burst of writing, day and night'. The word 'hundred' has been added in stanza 104. I have regularised the punctuation of dialogue, and punctuation has been added to the second line of the following stanzas: 9, 24, 25, 50, 53, 65, 77, 85, 104, 107, 111, 112, and 116. In addition, question marks have been added at stanza 23, line 1 and stanza 88, line 4, and a full stop at stanza 94, line 4.

p. 202 'To the Illegitimate of War': f.p. in *11P*. Source: Bod. Dep. Peake 10, fol. 9ʳ (MS). Date: A note in the source suggests the MS was 'Probably torn from notebook entitled "Nonsense II"' (i.e. Bod. Dep. Peake 5). This notebook contains an early draft of 'The Rhyme of the Flying Bomb', written on Sark c. 1947 (see previous note).

p. 203 'Truths Have no Separate Fires but from Their Welding': f.p. in *Poetry Quarterly*, vol. 10, no. 1 (Spring 1948), p. 4. Reprinted in *Gb*, p. 40. Date: f.p.

p. 203 'Poem: He moves along the bleak, penumbral shire': f.p. in *Poetry Quarterly*, vol. 10, no. 1 (Spring 1948), p. 5. Reprinted in *Gb*, p. 29. Date: f.p.

p. 204 'An Ugly Crow Sits Hunched on Jackson's Heart': f.p. in *The Wind and the Rain*, vol. 5, no. 2 (Autumn 1948), p. 95. Reprinted, revised, in *Gb*, p. 28. Date: f.p.

p. 205 'Poem: As much himself is he as Caliban': f.p. in *New English Review Magazine* (September 1948). Reprinted in *Gb*, p. 9. Reprinted in *SP* with the title 'Caliban'. Date: f.p.

p. 205 'Snow in Sark': f.p. in *W&D*, p. 86, with all alternative lines included, so that the poem is unintelligible. Source: MS. The last word of the poem is missing because the MS is torn; *W&D* gives it as 'sun', which does not rhyme and makes no sense; 'sea' seems the obvious reading. Comma added after 'tide'. Date given in *W&D*.

p. 206 'Poem: The paper is breathless': f.p. in *Gb*, p. 18; also in *Drawings* 1949, which was prepared but not published before *Gb*. Date given in *PP*, p. 252.

p. 206 'Conceit': f.p. in *RoB*, p. 21. Source: Bod. Dep. Peake 10, fol. 5ʳ (MS). Date conjectural. In Dep. Peake 10, 'Poem: The Paper is Breathless' occurs in an early draft, where the word 'yawning' is scratched out in line 1 and 'breathless' is substituted. 'Conceit' and 'Out of the Chaos of my Doubt' are written on the same greenish paper in the same brown ink, and corrected in black. I conclude that these three poems were all written by 1948, the date of 'Poem: The paper is breathless'.

p. 207 'Out of the Chaos of My Doubt': f.p. in *SP*, p. 10. Source: Bod. Dep.

Peake 10, fol. 4ʳ (MS). Date conjectural; see previous note.

p. 207 'To Live at All Is Miracle Enough': f.p. in *Gb*, p. 3. Date given in *PP*, p. 255.

p. 208 'The Old Grey Donkey': unpublished. Source: UCL Box 3 (iv), fol. 97ᵛ. Date: the date given indicates the period covered by the source.

p. 209 'As the Kite that Soars': unpublished. Source: UCL Box 3 (v), fol. 125ᵛ. Date: the date given indicates the period covered by the source.

p. 209 'Poem: What panther stalks tonight': f.p. in *Gb*, p. 21. Date: f.p.

p. 210 'The Rebels': f.p. in *Gb*, p. 31. Date: f.p.

p. 211 'Poem: With power supernal dowered': f.p. in *Gb*, p. 33. Date: f.p.

p. 212 'And Then I Heard Her Speak': f.p. in *Gb*, p. 34. Date: f.p.

p. 213 'The Flight': f.p. in *Gb*, p. 38. Date: f.p.

p. 214 'As I Watched between Two Forests': unpublished. Source: UCL Box 4 (iii), fol. 38ᵛ. Comma added at line 9. Date conjectural. The MS contains early drafts of chs. 12–15 of *Titus Alone*, pre-dating those in Box 4 (i), which is dated 1954–6.

p. 214 'Heads Float about Me': f.p. in *RoB*, p. 33. Source: Bod. Dep. Peake 12, fol. 1ʳ (MS). Full stops added at line 8 and 10. Date: the Bodleian document is entitled 'Poems Written at Virginia Water Hospital circa 1960–61'. In fact Peake was at Holloway Hospital, Virginia Water between March and August 1958.

p. 215 'Swallow the Sky': f.p. in *SP*, p. 8. Source: Bod. Dep. Peake 12, fol. 2ʳ (MS). Date: see note to 'Heads Float About Me'. Also dated 1958 in list of 'Possible Poems for Private Press' written by Gilmore.

p. 216 'Coarse as the Sun Is Blatant': f.p. in *SP*, p. 12. Source: Bod. Dep. Peake 12, fol. 3ʳ (MS). Comma added at line 11, full stop at line 12. Date: see note to 'Heads Float about Me', above.

p. 216 'Through the Voluminous Foliage of the Mind': unpublished. Source: Bod. Dep. Peake 12, fol. 4ʳ (MS). Punctuation added at lines 3, 5 and 7. Date: see note to 'Heads Float about Me', above.

p. 217 'On Fishing Up a Marble Head': f.p. in *3AQ*, no. 2 (Summer 1960), p. 6. Source: Bod. Dep. Peake 12, fol. 5ʳ (MS). Date: see note to 'Heads Float about Me', above.

p. 218 'Poem: That lance of light that slid across the dark': f.p. in *RoB*, p. 19. Source: Bod. Dep. Peake 12, fol. 6ʳ (MS). Date: see note to 'Heads Float about Me', above.

p. 218 'Poem: When I was wounded': f.p. in *RoB*, p. 9. Source: Bod. Dep. Peake 12, fol. 7ʳ (MS). Punctuation added at lines 8, 9, 10, 11, 13, 15 and 17. Date: see note to 'Heads Float about Me', above.

p. 219 'Poem: Out of the overlapping': f.p. in *P&D*. Also published in *New Poems 1965*, p. 129. Source: Bod. Dep. Peake 12, fol. 8ʳ (MS). Date: see note to 'Heads Float about Me', above.

p. 220 'Poem: As though it were not his, he throws his body': f.p. in *12P*. Source: Bod. Dep. Peake 12, fol. 9ʳ (MS). Date: see note to 'Heads Float about Me', above.

p. 221 'Break Through Naked': f.p. in *MEMG*, pp. 302–3. Source: Bod. Dep. Peake 12, fol. 10ʳ (TS), and another TS. Date: see note to 'Heads Float about Me', above.

p. 222 'Poem: Thunder the Christ of it': f.p. in *RoB*, p. 1. Source: TS. Date given in list of 'Possible Poems for Private Press' written by Gilmore.

p. 223 'Hail! Tommy-Two-Legs': f.p. in *PP*, p. 575. Source: MS. Date given in list of 'Possible Poems for Private Press' written by Gilmore.

p. 224 'Great Hulk down the Astonished Waters Drifting': f.p. in *3AQ*, no. 2 (Summer 1960), p. 7. Source: Bod. Dep. Peake 9, fol. 112^r (TS). Punctuation added at lines 10 and 11. Date given in list of 'Possible Poems for Private Press' written by Gilmore.

p. 224 'For Maeve: Now, with the rain about her': f.p. in Watney, p. 151. Source: MS. Comma changed to full stop at line 2; full stop added at line 5; comma added after 'breast' in line 8. Date given in MS.

p. 225 'An Armful of Roses': f.p. in *P&D*. Source: Bod. Dep. Peake 9, fol. 115^r (TS).

p. 226 'I Cross the Narrow Bridges to her Love': f.p. in *10P*. Source: TS.

p. 226 'My Malady Is This': f.p. in *10P*. Source: TS.

p. 226 'At Such an Hour as This': f.p. in *10P*. Source: MS.

p. 227 'Staring in Madness': f.p. in *10P*. Source: TS. The word 'rightly' is conjectural; the end of the line is missing in the TS, which is clearly based on a messy first draft.

p. 227 'For God's Sake Draw the Blind': f.p. in *11P*. Punctuation added at end. Source: TS.

p. 228 'A Presage of Death': f.p. in *11P*. Source: TS. 'In lamplight' is 'is lamplight' in the source, and I have transferred a quotation mark from the beginning of the sentence 'O Sunlight!' to the end of the phrase 'its remote singing'.

p. 228 'The Eclipse': f.p. in *11P*. Source: TS.

p. 229 'Lies! Lies! It Is All Lies and Nothing Else': unpublished. Source: Bod. Dep. Peake 9, fol. 19^r (TS).

p. 229 'Love Is an Angry Weather': unpublished. Source: MS. Full stop added at end.

p. 230 'O Love, the Steeplejack': unpublished. Source: MS.

p. 230 'She Lies in Candlelight': unpublished. Source: TS.

p. 231 'Than Paper and a Pen': unpublished. Source: Bod. Dep. Peake 9, fol. 23^r (TS). Punctuation slightly modified.

Index of Titles

Index of First Lines

254

FyfieldBooks

Two millennia of essential classics
The extensive FyfieldBooks list includes

For more information, including a full list of FyfieldBooks and a contents list for each title, and details of how to order the books, visit the Carcanet website at www.carcanet.co.uk or email info@carcanet.co.uk